Do Some

memora...

H...
Your Mind
-The 10 Best Ways-

Effective and Practical Methods to Help You to Survive and Thrive in an Increasingly Stressful World

Best Wishes,

Simon Ralph

By Jim Ryan and Simon Ralph

Eternal Point Publishers
eternalpointoflight.com

ISBN: 978-0-9935350-1-7
Eternal Point Publishers
Cover Design by
Pixel Studios

For Worldwide Distribution

Challenges, decisions, problems, difficult people, health issues, getting things done, commuting... it goes on... and... on...

Where is day light and clear water? In fact, where is your life?

So, how can we deal with all these major concerns that seem to be constantly battering at our door - and still have a life?

This little book will show you how!

It will show you clear and effective ways to deal with these issues. If you want to change your life but don't know how, then here's a good place to start. All this is only possible when you have a relaxed mind.

Through The 10 Best Ways, you will gain new, clear and insightful approaches that will give you confidence, strength and a new, deeper awareness.

Inside this book you will find personalised strategies on relaxing the mind, and the benefits of doing so.

This is training for your mind, your most powerful tool, enabling it to unfold and blossom.

When these guidelines are applied regularly, positive transformation is inevitable within your life. Peace becomes your natural nature, and life becomes a game again, in the same way it was when you were a child.

Each informative chapter concludes with a powerful and practical affirmation for relaxation that is simple, assertive, succinct and memorable. These affirmations encapsulate each section, and can be easily integrated into your life.

Learn how to replace negative thoughts and emotions, and become energised, empowered and confident.

This new mind-set pattern helps you to break old belief systems and to become happier, healthier and more relaxed in your life.

Peace and relaxation cannot be achieved in the outside world unless we master our minds and develop a level of peace on the inside.

If you are genuinely interested in freeing yourself from tension and knowing how to avoid stress, anxiety, and depression, and how to feel truly at ease and relaxed with yourself, then this book is a must-read.

About the Authors

Jim Ryan and Simon Ralph, co-authors of, *How to Relax Your Mind – The 10 Best Ways*, are both deeply interested in the human mind, and consciousness.

They are on a life-long spiritual voyage of discovery, and have a strong desire to grow their awareness on a personal level, and to help others to discover their true identity of Soul.

They do however, have very different backgrounds.

Jim is a former Principal, a teacher of teachers and management trainer. He is a long-time practitioner of meditation and spiritual study. His path has been through many ways, exploring the depths of Christian mysticism and the subtle arenas of psychic and spiritual experience to the practical strategy worlds of human development in both the educational and corporate worlds. "It's one journey, one direction and one destination," Jim emphasises.

Simon chose to see life from another perspective, that of global traveller, DJ, and once a Bus Driver. Amongst other adventures he has trekked the Himalayan Mountains, sailed the Caribbean Seas, backpacked the Australian Outback, and driven the perimeter of USA. But now, his journey is an internal one. An inner journey of realising the self, the drama of life we are in, and God.

He now focuses his attention on creative projects, on which he shares, "For me, creativity is the cutting edge of alive-ness. When I am inside the creative process, I am truly living..."

Strangely, both authors do have many things in common. Both have published books before co-writing together.
Jim Ryan is the author of *The Crystal Mind, Meditation The 13 Pathways to Happiness* and *In The Stillness.*

Simon Ralph also known as The Yogi Bus Driver released *Soul Journey of a Yogi Bus Driver* in late 2014.

Both study and practise meditation; both facilitate seminars and workshops; both teach and lecture on meditation; and both have experienced an awakening of the soul through spiritual knowledge, as well as having deep insights into the nature of the soul and God.

Together, they are complementary, well informed, and practical in their approach to living a full and complete life, using meditation as the foundation.

This book is dedicated
to World Peace
and a world where we
may all wake up to
the truth of
who we really are.

Chapters

Introduction

Introduction

Relaxing the mind is probably the most important thing we should do every day. But how much energy and attention do we give to this essential daily practice?

Once we understand that all of the stress we experience in life is created not, as it may seem, by the people around us, or the situation in which we find ourselves, but by our own response to these things. When we understand this, we can begin to see the importance of relaxing our minds.

Relaxing our bodies is something that we are both familiar with and used to doing regularly in everyday life. Most of us realise that if we push our bodies too hard, without relaxing every now and then, something will definitely go wrong!

Even athletes and sports people know that, in order to achieve greatness in their sport, they have to relax their bodies for a certain length of time.

The body only responds to training and exercise to an optimum level when this rest is balanced with exercise.

We also observe a state of relaxation in nature. Nature has a *'still point'* within its seasons, or cycles. It has times of growth, and times of quietness in preparation for the next spurt of activity. The relaxation of nature is, well, natural...

Are we able to relax in the natural way that nature does?

When we look at the mind, we can see that it is a very powerful part of who we are. The mind is very hard to locate, physically, that is.

Where, within your body, would you say your mind is?

Sometimes you can see where your mind is going. Sometimes it goes into the past or sometimes into the future, but you may notice that, rarely does it stay in the present moment.

The mind is non-physical, it is the thinking part of us, but it is not *all* of who we are. It is a very powerful resource.

It is the part of us where our thoughts are created. It is the production centre of our ideas. However, in these modern days, due to our fast pace of life, and the recent explosion of information available to us through the media, the mind is often scattered and fragmented.

So, how do I relax my mind?

Firstly, I need to make friends with my mind. It may seem quite strange that my mind would not be my friend, but ask yourself this: *Am I in control of my thoughts, or are my thoughts pulling me into places that I really don't want to go?*

This is the acid test.

If the answer is that your mind sometimes seems to play tricks on you, by sending you into unwanted thought patterns of worry, concern or fear, then this is not a true friendship.

It is a common occurrence to experience a negative downwards spiral of thinking.

Once in this destructive whirlpool of thinking, it can be very hard to come out!

Friends support and help me to achieve only beneficial goals in my life. They wouldn't disrupt my life, sabotage my efforts to live a good life or destroy my hopes of a positive future, would they?

Like a naughty child, the mind needs to be disciplined with love and compassion. It needs to be guided onto the right path. It needs to be controlled and focused, and steered in the appropriate direction, thus creating a suitable *train of thought*. It is in this *train of thought* that we can travel in the right direction and arrive at the correct destination. The destination of **Happiness** can then fill our lives, and the lives of others, with joy.

Happiness is one of our original qualities, and, as we now empower the mind, we can reclaim this treasure and align with this power.

The chapters within this book will help you to:-

1. Move into the world of happiness, and use it at every step and turn of your life's journey.

2. Examine the reasons why you are not able to relax your mind.

3. Unearth secrets, and implement methods on how to focus your thoughts and bring the mind back to a place of stillness.

4. Re-create your life afresh.

5. Discover ways to reinforce the habit of positive thinking.

6. Re-energize the soul through powerful affirmations that can be practised daily.

7. Become full of a lightness that is attractive to all.

8. Experience your full potential.

9. Understand the bigger picture of life, and help others to find their purpose.

With each way, there will be an affirmation of intent and awareness.

The affirmations talk directly to our subconscious, which is holding the fear. To make these affirmations really work effectively, try the three-step approach:

1. Read through the affirmation, acknowledging and accepting its message.

2. Then read it again, but this time, read it with feeling while experiencing the vibration and energy that the statement evokes within you.

3. Finally, integrate the affirmation's intention, absorb it, become it, and hold the feeling and emotion.

Chapter 1

The Way of
Dealing with Fear

Fear seems be a constant companion of most of us these days. It's become so much part and parcel of our lives, that without it, life would seem very strange indeed. Yet, when it comes, it creates the havoc of anxiety and doubt, sabotaging our joy, enthusiasm and determination, resulting in poor attitudes and performance, not to mention a plethora of health issues.

Everything seems to be set up for us to experience fear; there are always the constant warning bells, admonishments of.... if you do or don't do this, it will hurt you, burn you, kill you etc. It's interesting to note that most of these ifs, buts, don'ts and shoulds, are not what's actually occurring, but they are all about what might occur.

Yes, of course, we have genuine fears, but on close examination most are imaginary. Maybe we can see fear as:

Fantasized Experiences Appearing Real

We then keep hold of and develop these fears and they eventually transform into beliefs and personality quirks.

Maybe, as Theodore Roosevelt famously stated, "The only thing we have to fear is fear itself, nameless, unreasoning, unjustified terror, which paralyses needed effort."

SOLUTIONS

So to bring ourselves and our lives back to the clear and open water of mental peace and clarity, it's urgent that we rid ourselves of this insidious virus that completely blots out the sunlight of joy and well-being.

Let us consider that these fears, these obstacles, are like wild animals – and that they're actually cowards, who will bluff you, if they can, to see if you are afraid, and they will try to spring up at you. But, if you look them in the eye, they will slink away out of sight.

It's like the child who thinks there is a goblin behind the curtain, but, on turning on the light, sees the goblin is really a teddy bear. In the same way, when we shine the light of observation and awareness on our fears, they become something else.

So, let's face our fears, reappraise and transform them by:

Facing, Ending, Answering, Responding

We will now explore and experience a selection of ways that will effectively move us away from our numerous fears.

Fear is, most probably, our number one biggest enemy. Fear is the single most restricting force by which we are influenced in these times.

Our lives are often lived on the basis of fear. This may sound harsh, but if we were to look at our lives objectively, what is our biggest motivator?

Would it be abundance or scarcity?
Which one drives us to go on?
Is it knowing that our lives will be full of everything we need, or is it the fear of not having enough?
Enough money, enough time, enough love, enough freedom...?

Fear is paralysing. It freezes us in our tracks. Fear stops us from enjoying or achieving our hopes and dreams, and drains away our power. That is, our power over ourselves, not over others.

When fear is present, the ability to make the right decision is clouded or completely blocked. Fear distorts our views and erodes our self-confidence.

When it comes to creativity, fear is a huge obstacle. It empties the soul of light, and fills it with darkness and despair.

These are reasons enough to make us realise that we need to relax our fearful minds.

The Way to move away from the Fear of Fear

You're sitting alone, quietly watching TV, and the front door is suddenly thrown open. Your breathing speeds up, your heart races and your muscles tighten. After a split second you realise it's the wind, and that no-one is trying to break in. Yet, your mind went into overdrive, projecting and imagining demons, monsters or criminals. For that split second you were so afraid, you reacted as if your life was in danger, but, in reality there was no danger at all. Most of our fears (as we shall see through the following chapters) are the result of imagination. What the mind thinks and believes, the subconscious creates.

One of the solutions to certain fears is to repeatedly expose ourselves to the thing we are afraid of, ideally in a positive way.

Using this exposure therapy, we gradually bring down the physiological fear response until it's gone or is at least manageable. Avoidance is certainly not the answer. Try to do something that scares you – talk to a stranger in a lift, speak up in public, contact an old friend that you have fallen out with. But, do everything in small steps. Observe your response and measure it from 1-10, then you can watch the fear reducing, as this automatically dilutes it.

As Mark Twain states: "Courage is not the absence of fear, it is acting in spite of it."

Face it, see it clearly and you'll see it diminishing. Just have the thought: "I'm in control. I can deal with it, everything is okay."

The Way to move away from Phobia Fear

Our phobias can create acute fears that can be quite out of proportion to the action or object concerned. We can be aware that our fear is irrational, but at the same time be at a loss to reason it out.

This situation is not helped by others who do not regard the situation or thing as particularly threatening and so give little or no sympathy to such areas as: fear of driving; fear of heights; fear of confined spaces; fear of needles; fear of insects. And so on.

We are often presented with the *Reality Frame versus The Fear Feeding Frame:* thoughts like "... the plane is going to crash...," but I know it's not going to crash, however I keep thinking it.

Phobias have their origins in many possible areas, such as: incidents or traumas; learnt responses; genetics; responses to panic or stressful interactions. So it is useful to analyse the phobia to find the trigger, which can help to remove the emotional response.

It helps to remember the event or situation rather than the emotion. Thus we try to understand where the phobia comes from and how it arrives by talking to ourselves.

I know it's just my imagination, it's a silly childish fantasy, so I let it go, for I know everything will be fine.

The Way to move away from the Fear of Failure and Success

Here again, we are actively imagining what a new incoming change will bring. This often sabotages innovation and newness. So again we need to talk to ourselves.

If it's meant for me, I'll get the job.

A jigsaw piece will only fit into the place meant for it.

Failure is the springboard for success.

It was my qualities and talents that got me noticed, that got me the job.

I am able to successfully accomplish what is now being asked of me.

An initial lack of success is like a darts player teeing up the successful dart with one or two preliminary *'sighters'*.

It's good to remember that many successful individuals such as JK Rowling, author of the famous Harry Potter fantasy series, and the sprinter Michael Johnson, four times Olympic gold medal winner, had a lot of so-called failures and rejections before they achieved their success. Let's talk to ourselves...

I am able, I have ability.

I deserve and can handle whatever success may come, and if things don't exactly work out, I can handle that, and that's OK too.

The Way to move away from the Fear of Public Opinion

Sometimes we are stopped in our tracks by the fear or concern (real or imaginary) of what others are thinking about us, or whether they are approving of what we are doing. Again, we have to face and question this thinking:

Do others really have thoughts about me; aren't they more concerned, even obsessed, about their own needs?

We have to ask ourselves:

Do I care more about what people think than I do about the quality of my own life?

It is good to remind ourselves that it's generally accepted that most people respect individuals who stand up for themselves, who do and say what they believe.

An individual's reactive attitude and behaviour is about what's going on in them and has nothing to do with what I'm doing.

No-one else can know my needs or the direction I need to take. I have the faith and trust that the things I need to say, the steps I need to take, will be ones that will bring benefit and fulfilment to me and will gain appreciation from others.

The Way to move away from the Fear of Emotions

We often carry suppression programming from our childhood, or a macho, it's-weak-to-show-an-emotion, attitude to life which bottles up in us and traps us in an emotional straitjacket.

It's babyish to cry... grin and bear it, pretend you don't care... you shouldn't feel like that...

Emotion was seen as betraying a so-called weakness, showing you as a lesser person.
To escape this fear-fenced fortress, we just need to give ourselves permission to experience, to laugh, to cry, to dance and sing!

We can experience and express things in a different way by writing things down, singing a song, painting or making a model. We can tell ourselves that showing emotion is what people like to see. It tells them that we are natural and genuine, that we believe in what we say.

Emotional energies carry our truth and our intention. They connect, when a more rational approach fails to convince.

My emotions are a natural reaction to my choices and decisions, a reaction to my level of awareness and my ability to understand myself and my world around me. So, opening to my emotional energies, I connect to the energy field of the world and so all becomes well and all becomes good.

The Way to move away from the Fear of Sickness

Past experiences of being unwell – especially with some of the more severe types of debilitating illnesses – connect with what we know and see to create fear and dread. Avoidance and denial will not resolve this effect. Again we have to face up to and confront these often suppressed thoughts and feelings.

Again we have to talk to ourselves.

This illness is created by me, by my choice of lifestyle, foods and attitude...

It is important for me to remember that an illness comes in order to pass. When it is gone, I will be easier and lighter.

It's a warning I need to be more careful. Let me reassess the things I'm choosing to do.

By allowing my fears of sickness to keep manifesting, I start to mimic the illness, as if I have it already, so as to justify the fear. I have to stop such waste thoughts. Let me accept that I am not my body, that I am not the pain. Let me see myself rather as the point of light, subtle energy that animates my body.

This will allow my mind to become free, peaceful and at ease. On this basis I now can make positive conscious choices concerning my life and the well-being of my body. This will result in a greater state of mental and physical well-being and spiritual health.

The Way to move away from the Fear of Non-Acceptance

We all want to be liked and accepted, to be part of the group. When we are in the company of others, and are unsure of who we are and lacking self-acceptance and confidence, we often find ourselves looking over our shoulders thinking... *Do they like me... am I saying /doing the right thing?* We find ourselves in a constant state of fearful unease, causing us to act almost like a performing seal, trying to please and conform to what we think is acceptable and popular.

It's good to remember that people like and respect individuals who, in general, are characters; who speak up; who have opinions (especially, of course, if given with a smile); who are themselves. And people very quickly discover and reject artificial attitudes and behaviour.

The law of reciprocity (karma) applies very much to this area of acceptance. What I give, how I act and behave with others, so will be the return in kind.

If I give respect and regard, that is what I will receive.

When I show appreciation and give co-operation, so the same will be shown and offered to me. Let's try accepting ourselves as we are at this very moment. I really don't have to please anyone else. I know I am creative and talented and that I have a great deal to share with others.

I have no need or right to demand that others like, respect or accept me.

I know that, when being myself, all things will work out positively and naturally, because I love the world and the world loves me.

The Way to move away from the Fear of Dying

Experiencing or observing bereavement can be a huge trigger for our own fears of mortality and the unknown. It can cause the unleashing of a multiplicity of worries and concerns.

Compounding that is the attitude of modern society, that the subject of death should be avoided. The feeling being that it only happens to others and, if I ignore it, it will soon go away.

Yet, as with all fears, it will not just go away by itself. We do have to face this reality.

Carlos Castaneda says: "Focus your attention between you and your death without remorse or sadness or worrying.

Focus your attention on the fact you don't have time and let your acts flow accordingly." Living as if each act is your last act on earth will give your life strength and meaning. There won't be any time for fear.

We need to accept death. Death happens and will continue to happen. It is a reminder of the impermanency of things. When I am reminded that all things go, I can determine to make the best of things. I came with nothing and I will go with nothing, so let me use what I have in a benevolent and worthwhile way, then, at the end, I will have no attachments and no regrets.

One of the main aspects of the fear of dying is the question: What happens after death?

One belief is that everything is finished, everything is over. Okay, then, there is nothing we can do about it, so it's pointless worrying. A more positive and optimistic view is that we carry on. In this scenario, if we do our best, we can look forward to a heavenly reward. Or, another possibility is that spirit survives the deceased body, and carries its energy and personality into another existence.

If we align ourselves with a belief regarding what happens after death, that will help us move forward, away from the dark shadows of imaginative speculation. In that way, we will radically reduce a great deal of stress and fear regarding death

The Way to move away from the Fear of a Loss

We live in a world where it seems that the main goal and purpose of our lives is to accrue wealth and possessions that give us some kind of desired status, from which fulfilment and happiness are attained.

Whether you agree with this or not, it is a fact that huge emphasis is placed on wealth and status, as symbols of success and social acceptance. The consequences of having neither are continually rolled out before us, resulting in worries and stress in most of us...... *How will I live? What will others think of me?* .... and so on.

Once we buy into this game, the merry-go-round continues, for consumerism is ever the entrepreneur, wanting to increase its hold, and constantly changing the goal posts. It suggests that what was essential and what you accumulated today will be neither enough nor suitable for tomorrow. So we are left on a constant edge, trying to match, trying to keep up, and worrying if we can afford it.

Okay, let's face this phenomenon, this illusion of wealth. To allay these worries and fears that are centrally targeted on how we feel about ourselves and on our relationship with others, we need to re-appraise how we think and feel about ourselves and what we really need for life.

Some possible reappraisals:

I have all I need, within myself. I have the capacity to be peaceful, loving and content. I have the ability to make my life what I want it to be.

I realise happiness is not based on possessions, money or status. It's about what I think, who I am, what kind of person I am. It's about living my own truth.

Money and wealth are just energies, and, like all energy, they come and go. I have faith that the right things will come at the right time.

The Way to move away from the Fear of the Future

Most of our fears are not fears of what we know, but are fears from the psychological conditioning of fear itself. Like that fear of what might happen, not of what is happening now.

You are in the here and now, but, if your mind is in the future, an anxiety gap is created. You can always cope with the present moment, but you cannot cope with something that is a projection of your mind.

You cannot cope with the future. This creates unease, worry, nervousness, tension, dread and so on and on.

Fears of war, nuclear terrorism, world economic collapse, plague and epidemics, the Earth being hit by asteroids, collapse of social and political systems, climatic catastrophes and so many more, are all seemingly on the horizon and fed and developed by TV.

Anticipatory programmes of what would/might occur if.... are very realistic and are often set as dramatic film stories. It's a wonder we can ever get a good night's sleep. Such is the shadow that is cast over our very active imaginations.

Let's burst one of the main fear balloons connected with these scenarios:

These things happen. *No they don't. These things only happen in the movies.*

Let's approach life now in a more positive way by recalling the proverb:

"As you sow, so shall you reap."

If the actions I make in the present are good enough, then my future will surely be good enough, so I don't have to fear at all. A beautiful present assures us of a beautiful future.

If you make a practice of doing things that scare you or challenge you, the less chance there is that you are going to be afraid of what is on the other side of tomorrow.

You'll have the confidence that, whatever life throws at you, you will be able to face. The future is coming at you in every moment, and it manifests itself as the present. Therefore, allow what you're doing now to influence your future.

In today's world there are many pressing needs and many issues that need to be addressed, but why not trust in the resilience and innate goodness of mankind to resolve these.

My responsibility is to be sensible and peaceful and to be an example of positive action. Let me choose to live in the present moment, full of positivity and good will, and to have faith that the future will manifest accordingly.

To help integrate these aspects into my life, a simple affirmation can be used. This affirmation will enable me to bring in various strategies to deal with fear.

In your silent space, affirm several times the following affirmation, allowing it to influence your attitude and feelings:

Happily, I let go of past fears and failures, and I embrace new learning and understanding as I move forwards, towards wisdom.

Chapter 2

The Way of Making Effective Decisions

Decisions can often be very hard to make. Having to make decisions is a serious cause of not being able to relax the mind. When I am holding onto something too tightly, it becomes almost impossible to make the correct decision.

When this happens, it is good to stand back, and look at things from a different angle. Then we can open up to more possibilities by looking at the bigger picture.

The bigger picture is seeing the situation in its entirety. It is looking at the beginning, the middle and the end of any given scenario.

When I can do this, I become aware that, just because something doesn't make sense right now, it may well make sense later on.

In this way, I don't make my decisions based on the short-term outcome, but rather on the long-term benefits of the end result being a win-win situation for all parties involved.

In this way I am not blinded by my own desires, or the desires of others, but I am able to make a solid, objective decision based on values.

We make decisions nearly every moment of our waking day; every connection, interaction and every circumstance we connect with is like arriving at a crossroads and deciding on a direction, a stance, a particular way forward.

The outcome of our lives is totally dependent on our making the correct decisions. The heavy collateral that usually comes with all this is stress and anxiety. Anxiety comes when we recall past decision scenarios...

I just don't want to go through that again. Or as we view with trepidation the high mountain that we think is the issue to be resolved...

*What shall I go for? How am I to manage...?
There are so many implications... It's all too
difficult. I just can't decide. I'm not able!*

Sometimes it all becomes too much and many
give up this front line position of making the
decision and leave it to others to choose for
them. This can be fatal. What do others know
about me and my needs? Their choices will be
based on their perceptions and experiences that
have nothing to do with me.

We can often be overwhelmed by the
complexity of what we have to deal with and the
choices we have to align with. This worry and
the accompanying tension lock us up. We freeze,
we hold too tightly to the issue and it becomes
almost impossible to make a correct decision.

Making a decision is about understanding,
having clarity that something needs to be done
or achieved and then deciding what course of
action to take.

What often handicaps our initial attempts can
be our own confused, personal attitude and
vision; how we see things.

As Anais Nin says, "We don't see things as they are, but we see them, as we are."

Things like internal attitudes of anger and intolerance, prejudicial views, an antagonistic nature, frustrations and fears will spin us in a vortex of emotional upheaval and will certainly cloud our perception and choices.

For effective decision making, it is imperative that the first step should be the preparation of the mind. We need to move away from any heavy emotional influences in order for the mind to experience the clarity of clear water, so that judgement will not be impinged or swayed unnecessarily.

Initially, you need to switch off from the decision you are to make. You need to clear your thinking and relax. Maybe go for a walk or rest if you are tired. If you're going through some emotional experiences connected with another, try to make peace with that person. Even if only in your own mind, try to reconcile the issue.

Have something to eat (though not foods that will wire you up).

Try using a short visualisation/affirmation:

Visualise a calm beautiful lake and repeat to yourself: I am like the lake, calm, still and peaceful. Repeat it two or three times, hold and allow the feeling of equanimity and calmness to fill your mind.

It is important, before jumping into making a decision, that we step back, create some space and allow things to become clear. Often we make rash decisions, and live to regret them later. So, don't hurry. Just stay calm, relax, and then move on to make the decision.

Here are some useful considerations to bear in mind if you want to be able to make good decisions while maintaining a relaxed mind.

The Way of Focus

Give your whole focus and attention to the process. Don't mix in sauces and flavourings of other issues. The scatter gun approach will lose you direction and inevitably the correct decision.

If you are easily distracted, the following mind exercise will help. Let's call it the *Magic Door*.

Visualise in your mind a door. Go through it, and on the other side create/ picture a large beautiful lake. The sky is clear and blue. The lake is surrounded by flowers, with some ducks resting gently on the surface. There is a chair by the lake for you to sit on. No-one else can come through your *Magic Door* to this scene. This is your place, a space solely for you. You can come here whenever you have to think, or to make a decision, but only you! Here you are alone, relaxed and content. On your seat, now bring the issue to your mind. Here you can, and will, give it your full and clear attention.

The Way of Resolving The Issue

Okay, you are now in a good space. You are feeling calm and relaxed, so hold this state, this good feeling. Your mind should be in a relative state of quiet as you bring the issue or concern directly in front of you. But...don't think too much about it.

It seems strange that we shouldn't think too much. In doing so there is a danger of tying ourselves in knots with all our thinking.

When we think too much, a huge amount of energy is used up which drains and exhausts us. When we have the habit of checking every avenue, looking at it from all possibilities, leaving no stone unturned, we can easily, and usually do, miss the point.

Why not try another approach. At the moment of engaging with the issue, let go of it. Now tune into your intuition. For most of us our intuition is asleep. We have been relying on our logical, left brain for so long that we think it is always right.

So experiment. Trust. Try not thinking and allow internal responses to come. One, or several, may come powerfully. Hold them, weigh them up and trust your intuitive mind to align and guide you. You may be very surprised by the easy results.

The Way of Visualisation

A very important and powerful part of effective decision making is the aspect of visualisation. Once we have decided on what action/behaviour/attitude is needed to achieve our purpose, we need to inform and convince our subconscious nature that this is the right course of action, that this is the right thing to do.

The subconscious holds the power and the reins that we need to go ahead and accomplish the decision. If unconvinced, it will sabotage and deflect our way, through emerging doubts, fears or old negative memories. It could even create some illness as a delaying tactic.

Sitting in a calm, quiet space, we can emerge a picture. What does the result look like? How do I want things to be? For example, I can picture smiling happy faces; all issues and situations resolved; people co-operatively working together; my venture successful; me in the place I want to be.

When this is done with focused and clear awareness, the subconscious will receive and accept this and will immediately begin to co-operate and be a major driving force in its accomplishment.

The Way of the Decision Process

Once we have some day light on the issue and are happy with our initial decision, to enable us to move in a purposeful direction, we must examine several important factors.

We need to step back and ask ourselves: Is the decision and its eventual outcome still to my liking? Is it still of importance to me in the scheme of things? Will it be possible for me to effectively carry the decision through? What are the odds? If good, this gives us encouragement, if not, reappraisal.

What will be the costs in terms of energy, resources and relationships...? What's the time frame? After answering all these questions, is it still worth pursuing?

The Way of Creating a Plan

To make life easier, to help keep us on track and to avoid letting things slip, a plan is needed. How will things look? What will be happening on a short-term and long-term basis as a result of my decision? What action will be needed in the different phases? What support and cooperation will be needed from others? What lines of communication are needed to be set up to keep relevant people informed and on board?

Creating a plan keeps me relaxed and, to some degree, detached, and keeps me from becoming overly obsessed with my decisions. If I over-identify with my ideas, I run the risk of losing myself and eventually suffocating the initiative. It's good to remember that I am not my ideas or decisions. The decisions are secondary. I, the conscious being who makes the decisions, am primary.

This awareness will help keep us afloat as we navigate life's dangerous waters.

Have a plan B. If things go belly up, what will you do? This area needs careful thinking about. Go through in your mind possible scenarios that might occur and how you might deal with them. This is a well worthwhile exercise that will free up your mind from potential worry-filled, imaginary scenarios.

The Way of Managing Your Decisions

Decide on a strategy that you can manage and are happy with. Be flexible and be ready to compromise. Things, people and circumstances do, and will, change. Watch for signs and be ready to respond. Watch what's happening within a situation. Take in the whole thing with patience.

Then, once relaxed and stable, move in the correct direction. An important thing to bear in mind is that sometimes the best action is no action. There is a huge difference between being pulled into a situation against your own will and consciously steering yourself in exactly the right direction you feel is correct.

In all decision processes, there will be blocks and obstacles to overcome. Some will be obvious, so an approach plan is needed. Other types of obstacles might possibly manifest as a result of change, so you might need to be prepared to change your pace and direction for a while, while you resolve these new factors in the equation.

The Way of Acting Responsibly

Very much embedded in our decision making should be a concern for what the effect and the repercussions of what we set in motion will be. It is a universal law. Whether we believe it or not, *as you sow, so shall you reap*, is well known. It is what is known as karma: the law of cause and effect.

Whatever actions I put into the world, the energetic effect of those actions will definitely come back to me.

Included in the energy of actions, is also the energy of thoughts and words.

All of these come back like homing pigeons. To add to this, the energy that I put out may come back in a different form, and at a different time, but it will very much come back in equal amounts. So let us build into our decision making portfolio a proviso that any decisions will be based on bringing benefit and benevolence to all in whatever form that takes.

The Way of Learning from my Mistakes

If I start to make decisions based on a pattern, and problems are repeating, then I am not learning from my mistakes.

It does take some humility and courage to look at what it is I am doing, and to realise that my patterns of thinking are not working. Again, stay separate from the decisions, learn from them, change, and move on.

To get us on track, let's try the following:

Ready, Aim, Fire

Ready: It is about being motivated. What am I here to do? What do I need to do? What is important in the way I go about doing it?

Aim: My strategies. What exactly am I aiming to achieve? How will I go about achieving it?

Fire: Action! Refocus! Action!

To bring these concepts into our lives, we can practise the following affirmation. Let us repeat it slowly to ourselves releasing its meaning into our awareness.

I let go of all limited outcomes, I listen to my conscience and act responsibly to bring lightness into my life and the lives of others.

Chapter 3

The Way of Harmonising Family and Relationships

One of our biggest challenges can come from those who are closest to us.

Paradoxically, these challenges are also our greatest opportunity to learn and grow. They are our richest chance to get to the next level.

Being the master of my own mind, and knowing how to keep it relaxed, is invaluable when it comes to living with family or friends in harmonious relationships.

As I understand how to remain balanced no matter what is happening outside of me, not only do I remain free from tension and stress, but I am able to help those around me to do the same.

This then re-enforces the atmosphere in such a way that others are influenced by it, in a positive manner. The result of this is greater harmony in relationships.

We can see how the *whole* is created by the individuals within it. If I can be a guiding force, who silently, through my own *being*, not *just through my words*, can uplift and support the group, then the stage is set for a mind that is relaxed and calm.

When I demonstrate the following ideas within relationships with family and friends, wonders can be achieved.

The Way of Acceptance

If only I could find the right partner, I would be so happy. If only my parents would change then everything would be okay. If only my boss were more tolerant, work would be great. If only the children would behave better.... Oh, if I could just change everyone I would be so happy!

We become trapped when we look for fulfilment anywhere outside ourselves. How can we change these people?

The truth is that we can't, and the more we try, the worse it gets. If our happiness depends upon the actions of others we become a victim. We become disempowered and we lose direction and self-respect.

Let me try another tactic. Change my focus from the outside to the inside. The only true relationship is the one which I have with myself.

All other relationships are a reflection of this one relationship. If I am in high self-respect, if I love and appreciate myself, I will attract respect, love and appreciation from others.

Let me accept others around me, and not try to change them. Simply being the example of a person who is calm and relaxed and secure in myself will begin to relax and change the atmosphere.

Others then will be naturally influenced and pulled into that same energy field.

The Way of Approval

The pattern of our present relationships is very often closely linked with the relationships we had with our parents. As tiny babies we become aware of our parent's emotional pain and we try to make it right for them. We try to keep them happy so they will be able to carry on looking after us, thus it is a kind of survival instinct. This makes pleasing our parents very important. So our future relationships might go something like:

I will try to be what you want me to be if you will stay with me and give me what I need.

However, people can't always be what we want them to be and so we feel let down. We may then try to change them, or we give up and become resentful, or we leave and look for someone else who might give us what we need.

Do not interfere with another person's role. Remember, each person is playing their own unique part, and our part is not to make anyone else into what we want them to be.

More often than not, when others experience this pressure, they will eventually end the friendship, but probably not before a prolonged and bitter relationship.

It is only possible to make changes in a relationship if I myself am prepared to change the messages that I am sending to the other person. If I allow them to be themselves, accept and appreciate who they are and the way they choose to relate to me, they are then able to become relaxed and calm. They will not have to feel that they need to be somebody else for me.

The Way of Encouraging Integrity

This is the foundation for a relaxed mind. When I approach life from a position of integrity, I find that there is authenticity in my being, and not just my doing. The authentic lifestyle is natural and stress-free. It is me, being myself, no matter where I am, or who I am with. When I can be equal in all my dealings, I am able to relax my mind without worrying about pleasing those around me.

This evenness is a breath of fresh air for family and friends, as they can take me at face value, as they know that there will be no mood swings or hidden agendas.

If this is what I am projecting out, then this is what will come back to me and will become the 'norm' within the group.

Therefore, my aim is to set this very high standard, always.

The Way of Setting Boundaries

Everyone needs space. This is possibly the most important aspect in maintaining healthy relationships. A boundary or limit is the distance we can comfortably go in a relationship.

These boundaries exist at all levels of our being: spiritual, mental, physical, emotional. It's about knowing where I end and you begin. So until I know who I am and what I want, it will be impossible to know what is right or not right for me.

When I don't know who I am, I will certainly not be able to have a healthy relationship of any sort, because there will be constant invasions of boundaries. Personal limits will be blurred as boundaries become intermixed. Confrontations, irritation, impatience, intolerance and lack of empathy will rear their heads. Others will feel affronted, disrespected and taken for granted if we constantly cross into their territory.

It is important for us to check what behaviours and feelings we think create a problem in our interactions with others. We will find that it is in these areas that our boundaries are weak.

Wherever we have a boundary problem we will find evidence of low self-esteem. Poor relationships, unhealthy boundaries and low self-esteem go hand in hand. We will need to go back and face each area of personal weakness, using self-restoring affirmations to reverse the negative with a positive attitude. Here is an example:

People's lives are their own and are the result of their choices. I respect who they are and what they do.

The Way of Self-Reliance

Do not be dependent on any other person. Remain independent, yet united.

If I do rely on another for anything, be it for help and support, physically or mentally, or for entertainment, happiness or even money, I will, at some point, be let down. This will cause me disappointment, and possibly even bitterness will develop within the relationship. This bitterness, in turn, will damage the atmosphere between us.

Once the atmosphere is damaged, trust is lost, and when problems arise they become difficult to solve. If this is allowed to continue, disharmony will become rife, leading to a breakdown in communication. This marks the beginning of the end.

Having said all this, remain united with all, and continue to unite others. If what you are holding onto is not accepted or your idea is rejected, just let it go, for the time being anyway.

Ask the question: Is it really worth pursuing and persevering with what is detrimental to the relationships that you have with others? The time for new ideas will come if you just be patient.

The Way of Flexibility

Routine is useful, but it can be a killer as well.

Structure is good, and necessary, especially within a family in order to keep things working smoothly, but once it begins to take away happiness in a family, there is a problem. Staying flexible is the key to maintaining joy.

Change is like new blood, or fresh water re-energising our existence. Making actions, tasks or duties interesting and varied can be the difference between harmony and enjoyment or all hell busting out. This variation makes us feel alive, and creates enthusiasm.

Creativity starts with our thinking and flows into our being and doing.

Experiment with newness. Not, however, at the expense of others, but for the benefit of everyone, including yourself. In fact, especially for yourself!

Yet, when initiating any type of change, we have to get everyone on board.

"What do you think?"
"What's your opinion?"
"What suggestions can you make?"

These are all good and empowering questions to ask.

So, clear communication and dialogue are essential, with compromise and re-assessment part and parcel of the journey. Then, whatever the direction that is taken, all will be travelling co-operatively and with ownership.

The Way of Working with Attitude

As we all know and probably have experienced, relationships can be extremely complicated, often needing careful negotiating and handling, a bit like approaching a military campaign.

As with all aspects of life, in order to decide on the appropriate course of action, a stepping back from things and a thoughtful assessment of the issues and challenges ahead will give us a good deal of clarity and insight, and added success. Challenging and difficult situations will, no doubt, be created by family members, friends, colleagues or acquaintances, who, because of past negative experiences and past traumas, will display difficult behaviour by being demanding, intolerant, aggressive, bullying, blaming, manipulating or tantrum throwing.

However, we must not let such behaviour get in the way of our relationship with them. Try having the thought:

They are under an influence at present, what can I do or give that will help?

It may mean at times we will have to be less insistent, more accepting, tolerant and understanding, or we may need to step in with a smile and be assertive. We have to be what they are not.

Whatever we put into a relationship is what we will get out of it. It's interesting to observe that whatever we give, we will receive in kind.
If I am aggressive, they'll snap back at me. If I give respect, they will return it. Whatever I want in my relationship I have to give first. Everything we give comes back to us. If I'm not receiving what I feel I need, possibly it means I haven't given it, haven't shared it.

Here are some helpful magic words:

I'm sorry.
What do you think?
Thanks, I appreciated what you did/said.
I'd like your opinion on this.

The Way of Making Peace with Your World

Very often issues and conflicts that we have with others can be based on things that are very small and insubstantial.

Maybe it started from the way they styled their hair or the way they spoke.

The issues may be long gone or not important, but what still remains is the resentment or the rejection of that person, which sours our dealings with judgements of them.

So let's resolve to have a clear out of our conscious and subconscious memories of all these hang-ups and attitudes, whether real or imaginary, that we have about others. This will enable us to have more open and honest dealings with them and be at peace with ourselves.

Negative and critical thinking creates a heavy cloud around our heart, making us less amenable and pleasant and more prone to negativity and reactive behaviour.

Firstly, make a list of all those you have issues and difficulties with. Then every evening, sit in a quiet calm place with your list. Bring one person at a time in front of you. Ask yourself what the problem or issue you're having with them is. Resolve to finish it, there and then. To help in this reconciliation, note down two good qualities of that individual that you have noticed.

Next day, if you see that person, notice what first comes to your mind. It should be the qualities you noted down, not the negative, critical stance you held previously.

Naturally and automatically your relationship will improve and your general attitude and mental health state will reflect that positivity.

The Way of Positivity

They say that you can only see in others what you have in yourself. And that, what you do see in others you collect, and bring into yourself, and make your own.

If this is the case, then only see the good in others and, by doing so, you will become good towards yourself.

It's worth reflecting on how we try to improve and change our nature and behaviour. While we have some successes and some failures, we certainly don't want our failures publicised or aired abroad. We hope others will have some tolerance and take more notice of our improvements.

So why should we then home in on the weaknesses of others or focus on the behaviour that they are probably desperately trying to change and to rid themselves of?

In thinking a little about how we are trying to improve some of our defective traits and work in a more positive and pro-active way, it becomes much easier to appreciate and notice the positive elements in others. Articulate what you notice:

Wow, I see you're so much calmer these days...
That was incredibly thoughtful of you...

That was so kind...
**That was very generous of you not reacting
to what they said...**

This powerfully supports others on their journey
of change and reminds us of what we also need
to do.

The Way of seeing the Bigger Picture

Try seeing the bigger picture and it will certainly
alter your attitude to others and situations.
Everyone, in their own way, is trying to do their
best according to their capacities and
awareness, often against the odds, and the odds
are very often stacked against us these days.

Let's support each other by being there when
others might need us. Show appreciation, have
good wishes and positive energy. Let's have no
expectations of others, but let's show by
example what we feel should be happening or
expressed.

This can be challenging, as our ego always wants to correct and criticise. Example is always the best teacher, the best way to bring change and to give support. Try it and you will catch the feeling behind it.

Why not try working with the **100/0 Principle**? The *100%* is about taking full responsibility for your relationship. The *0%* is about expecting nothing in return.

Demonstrate respect and kindness, whether he or she deserves it or not, while expecting nothing in return.
Be persistent with your kindness and don't give up, remembering not to expect anything in return.

It's an interesting paradox that is happening here. When you take authentic responsibility for a relationship, more often than not, the other person quickly chooses to take responsibility as well and consequently the *100/0* relationship quickly transforms into something approaching *100/100*. What a breakthrough!

Remember the *100/0* Principle is about giving not taking; it's about the heart not the head, it's about kindness, respect and patience, it's about the little things making the difference.

After reflecting on the above ideas, it can be very helpful to bring all the points together into one very powerful affirmation.

This affirmation can be practised silently several times per day to reinforce you with positive energy, so helping your mind to stay relaxed when dealing with family and friends.

**We are all connected; we are all part of the same collective, universal family.
We each try our best, so let me be understanding as I support each one to laugh and smile as they find their way.**

Chapter 4

The Way of Keeping My Mind Relaxed at Work

Relaxing the mind at work can be tricky.

In society today, we are conditioned to stay alert and to keep thinking, and this is amplified multi-fold when in the workplace. Work is normally a place where we act differently from when we are 'not working'...

However, this very statement is the reason that we are not able to relax whilst at work! In fact, it is not about the place that we are in, or even the people that we find ourselves with, but rather it's the attitude that we go there with.

With this understanding, we can see that it is just a switch of awareness that can change our attitude to work.

We can create whatever we want to experience in life by changing our thoughts to correspond with what we wish to happen. In this way we take back control of our lives and, in doing so, we move away from societal hearsay attitudes and norms. It is our journey, our life, and we get to choose for ourselves the way things are, and how we are going to react to them.

Here is your tool kit of best ways to assimilate into your mind and so allow it to maintain an even level of relaxed alertness whether you are at home, at work or on the moon.

The Way of Maintaining Good Relationships at Work

How we get on with others, how we relate to each other in the workplace, can have a massive effect on our lives and emotional well-being. Minor irritations can escalate to major concerns and then into major confrontations. By altering and changing our mindset and attitude to our colleagues, we can easily avoid such scenarios.

Asking how things are going might clarify things more easily, though many prefer to keep such information to themselves.

Maybe they're going through stuff at home, difficulties with their partner or their kids. Struggling with payments, or a recent bereavement.

Seeing and thinking empathically changes everything and, of course, pulls us away from negative, critical attitudes and behaviour.

Try changing your attitude to others. Think rather that these are all my friends, my brothers and sisters. They are all part of the great family of mankind. Or, think of us all as actors, simply playing parts in the great drama of life.

These responsibilities, these roles we are all playing, are just temporary and not so important that we need to get upset about them. This moves me away from expressing superiority and arrogance.

The Way of Under-Promising and Over-Delivering

When we come from a position of humility, greatness unfolds. Humility is attractive. We are not talking about being a doormat here, but rather, living in our own self-respect. Embracing humility will enable us to make the effort to listen to and accept others.

It's interesting to observe that the greater acceptance of others a person has, the more that person will be held in high esteem and the more that person will be listened to.

One word spoken in humility has the significance of a thousand words spoken in arrogance.

So what is humility?

Humility is about letting go and letting be. The stone of conflict lies in the attitude of 'I' and 'mine' and in the possessiveness of a role, an activity, an object, an idea. Humility eliminates all this, enabling us to become dependable, flexible and adaptable.

Work without making false claims, or trying to impress. Seamlessly complete all tasks before they are asked for. Quietly go about your duties, seeing the beginning, middle and end of each one in full, before even starting.

Leave no room for complaints, and ensure that all *i's* are dotted and all *t's* are crossed. Have no expectations for recognition and praise, for this will only lead to disappointment and waste thoughts, which will surely come.

Work in such a way that is not competitive or showy, but in the end brings satisfaction to you and others.

The Way of Refraining from Gossip

There is so often a tendency to speak of others, especially while in the workplace. Sometimes this is done in the open, and sometimes behind backs.

As tempting as it may seem to pass on juicy gossip about someone, do not fall into this trap!

Once trapped, it can be hard to escape from such a dangerous hole! Gossip is not just friendly banter, it is poisonous and destructive, not only to the one being gossiped about, but even more so for the gossiper (and the listeners).

This negative energy pollutes the atmosphere and infects all concerned. It is an illness that spreads like a virus out of control. Gossip is an attention seeker and says more about the speaker than the victim.

When faced with this, let's not be passive, but rather hold our truth and stand up to these mind games.

"Okay, there may be a kernel of truth in what you say. Let's ask so-and-so if it's true," or, **"I feel uncomfortable talking about X whilst she is not in the room. Let's wait until she can be with us to continue this discussion."**

With this stance of courage and honesty, you'll feel so much better about yourself.

The Way of Avoiding Boredom

Of all motivational problems we encounter at work, the biggest may simply be just getting through the day.

The day-to-day monotony of repeated tasks can be extremely difficult to cope with. Boredom is partly due to insufficient stimulation and that problem is largely resolved by focusing on tasks rather than on time.

When we focus on the task in front of us, we forget about time, leaving us with no sense of the hours crawling by. When we are bored, we waste time and this makes time drag and things get even worse. Focus on making your work interesting; increase your motivation; stay busy.

Subdivide your tasks, so it doesn't appear you have a mountain to deal with. Play music; improve your work area; have pictures of family and things you like to make you feel more comfortable. In spare moments or breaks, *web browse (if permitted)* and entertain and enliven yourself.

Involve yourself in other tasks that are not your job, like caring for plants, coaching co-workers. Do things that create variety in your day which helps to fill dead time and can be rewarding. Try starting the day well, in a positive and enthusiastic way.

Begin with meditation, have a good breakfast, enjoy your commute, listen to a story or to music or have creative day dreams, planning holidays and so on.

During the day, drink plenty of water. Mental fatigue occurs when we become dehydrated. If we do get exhausted at work, have a short mental time out with some affirmations of meditation. If your boss allows, take a power nap to quickly energise.

When performing a task that you are not so keen on, focus on not minding that you have to do it...

Do not make a fuss about a situation or cause a problem for others. Instead, act as if every moment is your last, and that you need to make the most of every second.

Every second of life is valuable. If things are increasingly getting worse, maybe then it's a sign that you need a change.

The Way of Taking Responsibilities Seriously

When we become aware of values and adopt them as motivations for our behaviour, our lives and our interactions are positively influenced.

Today, the majority of people tend to define worth by material values such as social position, monetary levels, external appearance or possessions.

Yet, using and living with higher, spiritual values, we naturally move away from that closed world of selfishness and conflict. We open up to acceptance, generosity and care. So, to move towards well-being, harmony and inner peace, we need to make specific choices of what values to adopt.

Moral responsibility is to accept what is required, to honour the role which has been entrusted, and to perform conscientiously and to the best of my ability.

So firstly, I need to take responsibility for my own actions. Once I realise that I am creating the world around me through my thoughts, words and actions, I naturally take care.

When a role is played accurately, there is efficiency and effectiveness, which results in satisfaction and contentment at having made a significant contribution.

Until this understanding is grasped, we can often feel like victims, caught up in an unfair game. Some people always seem to get away with things, not contributing or co-operating and seemingly not having to pay the consequences for their deceit or wrongdoing. But such actions produce little or no job satisfaction, no feeling of inner well-being. Such negative behaviour only seems to produce feelings of emptiness and self-loathing.

Alas, the spiritual law of karma, *every action will have a reaction,* does not always take effect instantly. This doesn't mean, however, that it won't kick in at some point! Rest assured, it will. It is the presiding law enforcement officer of our world; the law of natural justice!

So it's important for us to consider the outcome of whatever actions we take, and the possible future effects on us and on those around us. This consideration is what makes it then possible to have a relaxed mind. With practice, integrity is built up, and becomes our guiding light. People who act with integrity are naturally loved and respected.

The Way of Being Respectful

Without respect among colleagues, the incidence of workplace conflict may increase, affecting productivity, morale, co-operative working and job satisfaction. All of which, of course, greatly add to the stress package with which we all have to contend.

It really doesn't matter whom you are working with, treat them as your equal, as you yourself would like to be treated. When speaking to others, try to feel that you are speaking to yourself, and imagine how it is being received.

We show respect by listening to others, being truthful with them, acknowledging and accepting their uniqueness.

Above all, speak politely, sincerely, and be genuine in your respect. On a regular basis, show gratitude, thank people for their assistance and support; a small thanks can mean a lot! Offer support and assistance, go out of your way to help, when it seems they need it, especially if it's not required of you to do so.

Respect others' abilities, not offering too much help, as that may sometimes be taken as disrespecting their ability to manage. Be a good active listener, learn to be quiet, maybe ask relevant questions to show you're engaged and interested.

When there is a need to respectively disagree, do so calmly and with tact, acknowledging common ground before adding your position.

If you can't say anything nice... keep a lid on it. It's not worthwhile being dragged into stuff that's of no value. Decide to like people, and then it's very easy to show respect. Yet at the same time, respect yourself, give yourself the same consideration that you give to everyone else. Don't short-change your own ideas.

Remember the Golden Rule:

Treat others as you yourself want to be treated.

The Way of Cultivating Tolerance

Good workplace relationships help you do your job better and can make going to work every day a joy. It stands to reason then that poor relationships can leave you demotivated. The aim of tolerance is peaceful co-existence.

While tolerance recognises individuality and diversity, it removes divisive masks and defuses tension created by ignorance. It's about adopting an open mind. It's about:

Training my brain not to judge people too harshly: For instance, a guy who can't decide what to order from the menu might be really good at solving complex financial problems. It is worth considering that I could just be plain and simply wrong about someone.

Acceptance: By choosing to accept that people are different, I can accept that different is okay and has no meaning other than simply different. To a large extent a person's behaviour is directed by and has originated from his/her situations. By situations, I mean things like family, friends, finances, education, culture, religion, values...

Priorities: If *good* workplace relationships are my priority, I can choose not to be bothered by many things happening around me that I don't necessarily agree with.

If I cannot change something or if something doesn't actually affect me, I can choose to hold no bitterness about it. If I am not concerned with being right about everything, I can let many things go, thus promoting harmony.

Accepting that I might not be as smart as I thought I was: Let's assume being smart is extremely important. People much younger than me have achieved much more than I ever will. I am definitely not very smart if I start comparing myself with the people I admire, rather than with the people I think are stupid.

Not having the right to criticise others: One should try to achieve something significant and meaningful (both at the same time) before one can begin criticising others. Until I do something truly remarkable, I should avoid judging others. I believe, however, if I do happen to do something great for this world, I wouldn't have the time to criticise others.

Not being a slave: If indeed I am surrounded by incompetent or stupid people and can't deal with them anymore - I should just get the hell out of there.

No-one has chained me to anything.

Not being too smart to not need anyone else:
While IQ is important, there are few things that I
can accomplish entirely on my own. If I can't
work with/for different kinds of people, my IQ is
of no use. Great leaders act like magnets for
attracting the top talent. One finger points the
way, but its five together that grasp the idea.

The Way of not making Assumptions

Very often assumptions are the cause of many
differences, divides and problems.

We allow presupposed conjecture, hearsay and
negative assumptions to stand unchallenged.

We jump to a conclusion without having all the
facts. As a result, we are, of course, being totally
unfair to ourselves and others.

To use the **traffic lights analogy**, we ignore the
green light messages in our lives. We make the
assumption that things will not change.

We assume the worst and, even when people give us a *green light*, we continue to react as if we had been given a *red light.*

Making assumptions is like having a veritable chip on my shoulder, assuming that people, things or events will go wrong. People will perceive me as sullen, angry and negative. By assuming the worst, we give our power away, allowing other people, things or events to easily upset or bother us. Negative power then begins to control us.

Acting in a stereotypical way, making assumptions about how someone or something is always going to be, we allow little flexibility and spontaneity into our lives and so become blocked and trapped.

By assuming that the worst is going to happen, we subconsciously set things up so that they do happen and in just the negative way we predicted. Most of the assumptions we reach are based on irrational thinking. The possibility of change is often not considered.

This self-sabotaging behaviour will stifle and strangle my growth, happiness and success, and will inevitably lead to failure and loss at every level. So let's decide to stop this negative cycle.

Let's decide to be optimistic and open ourselves to life's Yes messages. Let's take back our power and not allow our past or others to influence us. Let's develop the habit and practice of rational thinking. Let's open our minds to truth and reality, and visualise success and positive results. Let's become spontaneous and carefree. Let's never be surprised about what happens.

Open your mind to all possibilities and move outside of duality in your thinking. Up and down, right and left, in and out, are only perceptions. Good and bad are only limited ways of seeing an event. Something that may seem bad right now, may be necessary to happen in order for the future to be a better place. In the same way, a good thing that happens may turn out later to be *not so* good.

Accept what you see with your eyes and hear with your ears, knowing that there may be something very different behind them.

The Way of Having Fun

When things get us down or get a little monotonous, being bored and fed up becomes the norm. Instead, try to bring some humour and fun into the workplace.

When we're laughing and having fun, everything changes. Endorphins and dopamine, the body's natural *feel good chemicals*, are released into the system, so we feel physically better as well!

Having fun reduces anxiety and tension and is the killer of stress; it takes the mind into a better space. Try to initiate a fun culture where you work. Celebrate events, successes and birthdays with food and drinks. Hold group activities, exercises and games at lunch time... table ping pong or Xbox, all help everyone to relax, bond and enjoy themselves.

Other examples of fun are: scavenger hunts, joke board/time, time-out places to relax, meditate or nap. A fun/laughter culture really helps to move towards a work/life integration.

It helps with colleague bonding, reinforces a group identity, increases friendliness and you become a more real person in the eyes of your colleagues. You begin to learn about each other and each other's needs, and, very importantly, it neutralises negative situations and emotions. It's about bringing newness and change. Change your seating arrangements, allow different people to collaborate or host an event inside or outside the workplace.

Fun and laughter help against burn-out, make the atmosphere exciting, challenging, and work becomes not such a bad place to be!

The Way of Considering Your Thoughts

As the saying goes, *the forest shapes the trees*, so the workplace shapes the person, the workplace shapes the performance.

Where you work and spend many hours each day of your life will have a considerable influence on how you feel and perform.

It's worthwhile, even essential, to change the workplace environment to ensure that it's a nice place to come to each day.

As much as possible, introduce more relaxed, personal and friendly influences. Choose restful, effective and suitable lighting, and chairs that are comfortable. Have decor and colours in soft and neutral shades.

Appropriate plants and pictures can support a culture of a creatively and relaxed working style. Maybe try to limit the noise and clatter of machines, phones and equipment, with carpets, wall linings and sound absorbent materials. Limit your clutter.

Work and workloads can take over our lives. It's good to remind ourselves that we work to live and do not, in fact, live to work.

Occasionally, step back and check your motivation, and your reasons for work. Am I living to work, or am I working to live? What is important to me? What are my priorities? What are my goals? What is my purpose?

Such reappraisal helps us take in the bigger picture of life... it's only a job... it then becomes easier to let go and stop holding things too tightly, which is exhausting and draining.

My job, the work I do, is only one part of many things in my life. Let's not become overly dramatic or obsessive about it. Let's let go of all the tension, worry and stress and allow our minds to become more easy and relaxed.

After absorbing the thoughts and suggestions above, of ways to stay relaxed but alert while at work, it may be helpful to repeat the following affirmation in your mind.

This affirmation may well help to crystallise the concepts in order to bring them into a living form within your life.

Step again into your inner world of quiet, and repeat the affirmation, reflect and experience:

As I remain light, easy and centred, I let go of (the situation / relationship), understanding that everything is held in the natural harmony of peaceful unity.

Chapter 5

The Way of Maintaining My Health

This is an area that we often neglect or take for granted, until, of course, things start to go wrong. Then, certainly, all our attention is focused on getting well and getting back to a normal life.

It's interesting that most of us tend to not think too much about health and health issues.

Is it a repression of a deep, subconscious fear, much on the same lines as thoughts about death – 'if we don't think about it, it will go away'?

Increasingly we are being made aware of our health, bombarded incessantly by a *media* hell-bent on selling us ways to cure, avoid, maintain or improve issues of the body.

More and more information and research is telling us that our health is, yes, certainly affected by food and lifestyle, but, probably more importantly, it is affected by the way we think. We need to take note of how thoughts, intentions and attitude affect our bodies and of how our bodies directly reflect what kind of thoughts we have.

So, it is vitally important that we learn to keep our minds in a calm and non-reactive state, otherwise strong feelings, such as fear, worry and tension will reverberate and ricochet around our inner body causing havoc and chaos on our health.

Health plays a major part in the overall picture of well-being. When even one small area of health goes out of harmony, we can experience great turbulence and distress; sometimes completely being put out of action. So, while not being obsessive or fanatical about it, health should be a major concern for us. Each area of our health should be approached with great respect and attention. Here are some *best ways* of maintaining health.

The Way of Mind over Matter

Whatever I think and feel will have an effect on my body. If my thoughts are heavy with fear and worry, then there will be locations in my body where these effects will be experienced. Repeated worries and negative thinking will eventually lead to some form of ill health.

Yet, there is a way we can deal with this, a way to go beyond the physical effect and discomfort.

Wherever I focus my mind, which actually works in similar fashion to a high-powered lens, that is where my attention will go. This seems obvious, and many would probably be in agreement. Therefore, if there is an illness in one part of my body caused by negative and waste thoughts, it would make sense for me to send positive energy through my mind to that place, to counteract the cause.

The mind is creating thoughts all the time, but if the thoughts are weak or fearful in regards to the illness, healing cannot take place.

Practise sending positive thought power to the illness or difficulty regularly, and this will enable recovery to take place.

The other side of this idea is that, if there is intense pain in one area of the body, take a break from it by moving your awareness away from that place for some relief for a period of time. Come back to it later, and again send positive healing thought-energy to the painful area.

The Way of Settling Old Accounts

As you may have already experienced before, old injuries seem to come back to haunt us in later life. Sports injuries for example, that took place when we were younger and fitter, and fearless and carefree, often can stay with us for life, and only begin to become a problem as we get older.

These sorts of injuries can be frustrating and are definitely able to stop our mind from being relaxed.

However, if we can look at things from a different perspective, we can see that these experiences later in life are the results of our earlier actions.

We cannot go back and change those actions, but we can change our attitude towards them. This, in itself, will change our experience.

The same principle can be applied to any injury we have, and indeed any dis-ease we experience. We may not be able to change the illness as such, but, by relaxing the mind, we can change the experience. The antidote for this is acceptance. We give ourselves space to assess and think clearly about what steps we can take. Also we are in a more receptive state to receive outside advice and more likely to act on any good suggestion.

The Way of Not Complaining

If I complain and constantly grumble about an issue, I increase it and make it worse by adding negatively charged thoughts to it.

As noted, the body and mind are interlinked, so there is a need to tackle the root of the complaint first in the mind. And if negative, self-pitying thoughts start to manifest, try not to express them through words.

This takes a little practice, but, with patience, we can steer ourselves away from the complaining habit. Interestingly our complaints can also affect others directly and also our relationships with them. No-one wants to continually hear a litany of woes and health conditions. It's depressing, as well as reminding everyone that ill health may be just around the corner for them too.

Instead of filling the atmosphere with such negativity, which brings everyone down, why not try and maintain an environment, an atmosphere, of lightness and positive well-being? Yes, it's a challenge, but these subtle efforts will certainly help us in recovery. By adopting such an attitude, it brings benefit to everyone.

The Way of Learning

Everything that comes to us is a life lesson, so, when a health problem arises, I need to ask myself what the lesson could be.

Sometimes, an illness may come that will change my entire life, thinking, surroundings and future. This can often be for the better!

There are always lessons to be learned. I may need to learn a lesson concerning my lifestyle. It could be something in my lifestyle that is causing the disease, something that I need to change.

Occasionally, a lesser illness comes as a warning sign that prevents a more major situation from occurring.

Everything is for a reason... Constantly my body is talking to me, sending signs and signals, trying to keep me aligned and on the right track. So it's imperative I stay alert and pay heed to this inner voice.

What does it mean? Why is this pain occurring? How should I respond?

It may mean checking with others more experienced in reading these reactions. That is part of the way we learn, the way we progress.

The Way of Food and Nutrition

Sometimes we can get a bit lazy or careless when it comes to nutrition for both the body and mind.

While this may be okay for a while, eventually it will catch up with us, and the consequences are always high. While not being too obsessive or fanatical about it, what we put, or don't put, into our bodies should be a major concern for us. *We are what we eat,* as the saying goes.

Luckily for us, a great deal of research has been done on what can be harmful and what type of things the body needs to function at an effective level. Maintain a balanced diet; watching out for possible imbalances of certain foodstuffs.

Not too much starchy foods such as cereals, rice, potatoes or pasta. Have a regular intake of fruit and vegetables. Cut back on saturated fats and sugars in your diet, like cakes, cheese, biscuits or cream. Certainly eat less salt. Avoid foods with trans-fats.

There are a required level of vitamins and minerals needed to keep the body in good shape, so keep a check on these.

Eat well and eat regularly. Don't go hungry, as this could lead to binge eating. Be flexible, often rigid diets will not work for all.

Change your portions, gradually cut down. Have more servings of vegetables. A better option would be to snack on healthy foods through the day.

Keep your kitchen stocked with lots of healthy options. Check your weight periodically to see how things are going. As good food and nutrients are good for our bodies, the nutrients for the mind are positive thoughts, good wishes and calm feelings.

We need to feed both the body and the mind to keep them healthy. With a little attention, it is easy to find the right balance, and live a good and long life.

The Way of Maintaining My Mental Health

I respect and honour my body when I work in harmony with it. This is only possible if my mind is relaxed. This state of relaxation is beneficial to the health and well-being of the body. The mind and body work as a team, and the soul, my true inner being, oversees them both.

Looking after my mind is then important and imperative. Let's look at some ways to keep the mind healthy.

Be Optimistic and Hopeful: Pull away from doom and gloom scenarios, look for the positive avenue. Things can't and won't always stay as they are. Change for the best will come.

Stay Connected: Staying close to and valued by others is a fundamental need and one that contributes and promotes inner well-being. So take time out to spend time with others in meaningful relationships.

Accept your Self: Ignore the media mantras of not being good enough, thin enough, rich enough. Look in the mirror and *say I'm okay. I'm doing fine and getting better all the time.*

Giving: Giving and sharing creates a great feeling of well-being and satisfaction. Do something for friends or for your local community. Helping others creates a tremendous bounce-back effect on our own happiness and well-being.

Express Gratitude: Find something to be grateful for in every situation. Showing appreciation reminds us of the goodness in people and situations and pulls us away from criticism and negativity.

Keep Learning: The mind thrives on newness and new experiences. Learning new things enhances self-esteem and encourages social interaction and a more active life. Do crosswords, research something unusual, learn a language, read a book.

Enjoy the Moment: Be in the now, notice things around you, where you live, appreciate your environment and the things in it. Notice others, their qualities, the things they do. This stops us falling into the past, trawling through what might have been or should have been. This helps to reaffirm our priorities.

Regular Physical Activity: Keeping the body active helps to pull us away from depression and anxiety and helps us to feel good.

By knowing that all the health issues that come to me make me experienced, helps me to maintain a relaxed mind.

This experience helps me to grow, become strong, and also to be of help to others when they are going through something similar. I am then an authority and so can support others.

The Way of Pain Management

Pain is the body's way of letting you know that something is wrong. Acute pain, if left untreated, can lead to chronic pain, which can be incredibly disabling.

Managing pain is, in fact, something that we can do with the mind, by keeping it relaxed.

As I reduce any tension in the mind, I am able to focus the mind on pain relief. Letting go of pain from the past, or the memory of pain, is the first step. As this reduces, I have the strength to direct the mind away from the pain of now. I can further concentrate my mind by letting go of any future pain that I may be worried about. As I stay present, I give more strength to the mind, so that it can stay in the now and deal with what is needed right now.

A simple exercise to guide our thinking and to relax the mind, and so move us away from the pain we might be experiencing, is to visualise a bird gliding gracefully high in the blue, distant sky. Now repeat this affirmation, slowly to yourself.

I am like a bird, free, light and detached. Sailing high above my body and all things below.

Repeat it, experience it, and then just hold that feeling of being free. Slow, focused breathing can also be a great help in easing the tension and tightness in the body. Fill with air from deep within your abdomen and then let it out slowly like a deflating balloon.

Buy yourself a joke book, or watch some really funny movies and laugh. Apart from cheering you up, laughter boosts chronic pain relief by releasing natural, healing endorphins into our bodies (as, of course, does exercise!).

The Way of
Being Aware of Influences

At this moment we are living in the middle of an electromagnetic soup, bombarded on all sides by electromagnetic fields, such as ELFs, radiation waves emitted from the countless electrical devices.

We are all using, the connecting Wi-Fi towers, plus the increasing dangers from leaking nuclear facilities. These are all contributing to innumerable health issues, such as cancers, tumours, fatigue and dizziness.

This is one of those areas that we know is dangerous and that has negative effects on us, yet our addiction and dependency overwhelm our sense and judgement. All this is not helped by the more subtle influences of negative atmospheres created by all our fears, anxieties and negative lifestyles.

After a while it all gets too much to think about, making us feel as if everything is harmful to us. Whatever we do, wherever we go, whatever we eat, is slowly contaminating and poisoning us.

So what can we do?

While we can and should think about such things, we need not dwell too much on them. Rather, let's be optimistic and take precautions, such as not exposing ourselves unnecessarily to these effects. Use your speaker rather put your phone to your ear.

Keep your devices away from your person as much as possible. Try not to live near a Wi-Fi tower. On the market, you can find protective devices such as pendants and shields that can help. Take iodine as a support and remedy when experiencing atmospheric radiation effects.

Regular meditation helps to create a powerful energy field of positive, protective vibrations, plus giving you the boost that it's not all going downhill, that you're dealing with it and that it's all going to be fine.

Taking care of the body allows the soul (my deeper inner being - me) to make the most of my time in it.

With this level of respect, the body stays healthy and in working order, and is available to be used for any activity that I ask it to do. In this case, the mind is able to stay relaxed, the body healthy and the soul happy.

The Way of Maintaining Balance

On the outside, it is important to keep the balance of home life, work life and social life.

If any one of these is out of balance, it will definitely affect my state of mind. I need to keep a good balance of exercise, rest and food as well. But it's my inner world that is often neglected. Unless I give myself time to relax, reflect and meditate, my mind is not going to be on my side.

The time that I need to give to unwind is crucial if I am going to create a good, strong, solid platform to live my life from. Try not to forget your inner world, otherwise you will be the one to pay the price as it manifests into a mind that is far from relaxed.

The Way of Determining My Outlook

Even if you think your future looks bleak, you can decide to create it to appear bright. For it is in the mind that your future begins. You can create a bright future if you set your mind to it.

Creative visualisation is a great method to manifest the future you want.

Project your mind into the future that you want to have. Give energy to that future becoming your reality.

When this is practised regularly, with enthusiasm and focus, you will eventually walk into that creation. This practice takes patience, but it is definitely possible to design the life that you want when you are able to relax your mind.

Now that we have covered a few suggestions that may be applied to supporting the health of our mind and body, let's take a few moments to crystalise this awareness.

Firstly let's read the affirmation, secondly then experience it, and thirdly hold it and become it.

**Stepping into my silent, inner world,
I let go of anxiety, pressure and fear,
In this inner, peaceful oasis,
My mind relaxes, and becomes empty,
peaceful and calm.**

Chapter 6

The Way of Effective Communication

Effective communication is probably the most important of all life skills. It helps us in every aspect of life, from our professional life, to social gatherings and everything in between. Good communication is about showing meaning in what we say and how we say it.

A common cry heard in many interactions is: *Say what you mean!* It sounds so simple, but all too often, what we try to communicate gets lost in translation despite our best intentions.

We say one thing, the other person hears something else and misunderstandings, frustration and conflicts ensue.

Fortunately, you can learn how to communicate more clearly and effectively.

Whether you're trying to improve communication with your spouse, kids, boss, or co-workers, you can improve the communication skills that enable you to connect effectively with others, build trust and respect, and feel heard and understood.

Communication is about more than just exchanging information. It's about understanding the emotion and intentions behind the information.

Effective communication is also a two-way street. It's not only how you convey a message, so that it is received and understood by someone in exactly the way you intended, but it's also about how you listen to gain the full meaning of what's being said to you and how you make the other person feel heard and understood.

More than just the words you use, effective communication combines a set of skills.

These include nonverbal communication, engaged listening, managing stress in the moment, the ability to communicate assertively, and the capacity to recognise and understand your own emotions and those of the person with whom you're communicating.

Effective communication is the glue that helps you deepen your connections to others and improve teamwork, decision-making, and problem-solving. It enables you to communicate even negative or difficult messages without creating conflict or destroying trust.

A relaxed mind is the optimum starting point of all good communication. However, a relaxed mind has become a rare place in which to be. The result of this is that communication has become disjointed and misunderstandings are common place. Such is the world we live in today, but it hasn't always been like this!

Myth has it that, once upon a time, all communication took place through the mind alone, and that words and sounds were just for entertainment.

Some say that one day it will again go back to those times, but for now, let's look at a few methods to communicate on a more physical level. We will explore some Best Ways to help make communication relaxed and easy.

The Way of Clarity

Clarity is of the upmost importance in order for an exchange of ideas to really be understood. There is nothing as infuriating or confusing as when things aren't clear.

Use simple, concrete language. Try not to bring in any unnecessary detail.

Express your ideas through fact and anecdote and don't be afraid to rephrase until you're understood. Before your meeting, order your thoughts.

Why not create a plan, write it, essence it, so you have it easily at hand? What's the main thing I want to get over? Are my facts all correct? What outcome do I want? Rehearse...

Correct pitching of your communications is essential. With a calm and easy mind, I can feel the pulse of a situation. This will allow me to find the right level from which to communicate.

Too high and anything shared will go over the heads of others, and I will be wasting my time and theirs.

Too low and they will lose interest and become bored. Catching the vibrations of the other person or people is possible when I am in a state of relaxation in my mind and body.

Think about the role and approach you're adopting. Is it helpful or confusing? If you suddenly decide to adopt an ambiguous manner that others are not used to, this can be confusing and possibly stressful for them. People often have a perception of how we should be and, when we move away from that, they become confused and suspicious. We always need to try to understand how others see us.

Don't use sarcasm or be cynical in communication, even if it is in jest. Loading my communications with sarcasm is a sure way to pollute the relationship and limit the possibilities.

Sarcasm is, as they say, the lowest form of wit. If I am putting anyone down in my communication, I am being foolish. Foolish because the energy that I am projecting is subtly negative and tarnishes the atmosphere. When the atmosphere is damaged in this way, communication becomes twisted and dysfunctional.

This is how misunderstandings are created, by saying one thing, and meaning another, just for the sake of base-level humour.

The Way of Credibility

One of the key ingredients to effective communication is credibility. No matter what is said, it's not going to make much difference in the mind of the listener unless the speaker is credible and believable.

So it's essential for us to build these two aspects into everything we communicate.

In all our dealings, we need to be authentic and to show authenticity. We need to be genuine. You are or you aren't. What you value is what you give. What you say is what you believe.

It's about being natural and being ourselves, and not adopting false personalities and playing games with people and issues; it's about going straight to the point.

We gain credibility when we show respect for another's position and ideas, when we welcome feedback and opinion, when we focus on possibilities and compromise.

It might seem obvious to say, but, if I am not available and accessible, no-one is going to communicate with me. Having a mind that is stressed and full of tension is like carrying a mobile phone around in your pocket that is not switched on; you're just not receptive.

So, switch on your availability. Be ready to receive. Don't to be so preoccupied with yourself or your problems and troubles that, even when someone is knocking at your door and calling through the letterbox, you can't even hear.

Be accessible, ready to help or support your fellows in their moment of need, or to be helped or supported by them in yours.

People tend to trust people who show concern and respect for them. They have to feel your concern, before they feel your words. Being genuine, being yourself, means you won't have to be concerned about how others are receiving you.

If I am trying to be too clever, it will be obvious that I am acting from an ego perspective. This will be an unsteady start to my communication. It will cause tension in my mind, which, in turn, will cloud my thinking, making it even harder for me to express myself clearly. Keep it simple, keep it succinct and keep it honest. Honesty shines through and enables a beautiful exchange to take place.

Honesty is the basis of a good relationship and will encourage openness and keep everything real rather than superficial.

The Way of Body Language

What people see and how they perceive what they see has a massive effect on how much of what you are saying they take on board.

Communication is largely non-verbal. Body language, including facial expressions, gestures, eye contact, posture, the tone of voice, and even muscle tension and breathing, speak louder than the actual words being said.

The way you look, listen, move and react to another tells them more about how you're feeling than words alone ever can. Understanding and developing non-verbal communication can greatly help you to connect with others; express what you really mean; navigate challenging situations and build better relationships at home and work.

You can improve effective communication by using **open body language**: arms uncrossed, standing with an open stance, sitting on the edge of your seat, **enhancing your message**: patting a friend on the back while complimenting or pounding your fist to underline your message.

One of the most important aspects of body language is the use of gaze, the way we see and use our eyes. Gaze indicates willingness to communicate or not. Prolonged gaze can be used for emphasis; too long gaze shows either intimidation or intimacy. High gaze can portray dominance or aggression. Shorter glances or increasing gaze can be used to signal we're finishing.

We need to synchronise and align with the words we are saying. For example, don't be saying yes while shaking the head indicating no. We have to be very aware of the signals we are giving and also learn to decode signals from others, thus helping us to improve, conform and change course if necessary. Thus, our communication becomes relaxed, effective and successful.

The Way of Good Listening

Everybody wants to talk, few want to listen. We will find ourselves poor communicators until we make up our minds we want to become good listeners. Listening requires a conscious effort and a willing mind.

Listening keeps me tuned into what's happening and better informed as to what needs fixing or changing, thus reducing the risk of inter-personal conflicts. This is especially helpful in the work place, helping to create an environment of peaceful well-being.

Careful listening to different ideas and points of view helps me to make better decisions. It increases my impact when I do speak. It gives me power, influence and a negotiating edge. It shows respect, care and humility. People feel appreciated, and it invites love and respect.

By creating space, by creating thinking time, stress and anxiety are reduced. This greatly increases successful interactions.

Listen compassionately. Listen empathically. This takes more than just giving glib assurances. When such an accepting atmosphere is created, people are empowered. They are enabled to lower their defences, to be less aggressive, to share truthfully and to find their own solutions.

Effective listening is about maintaining good eye contact. It is about showing commitment and empathy through positive body language. It is about feeding the other's content by endorsing key words or phrases, by building on their content and not deviating or side-tracking into my own interests.

Focused listening is about catching all that is being said. However, it is also about being able to decipher what is left unsaid, or is only partially said. Focused listening will help a nervous or inarticulate speaker link together pieces of their dialogue to make it more focused and clear. Effective listening allows the speaker to use silences or long pauses. Because there is no hassling and pressurising for immediate and concise information, the speaker is given a chance to comfortably gather their thoughts, to reformulate, if necessary, and then to carry on.

Good listening is when we check our understanding, isolate key features and ascertain the main intentions of the speaker.

The Way of Persuasive Communication

When we have something to say, we often spend as much time in worrying how others will take it as we do in preparing our topic.

There are three main ways of being persuasive.

1. Logical reasoning.

2. Working with and appealing to human goodness.

3. Working with emotional energy.

Here are some quick pointers to good persuasive communication.

• In most situations, identifiable emotions may carry as much, or more, weight than logic. So it's worth taking time to decide which emotional position or slant to take. Focus on generating positive feelings and emotions, always aiming to leave the other party feeling happy and satisfied.

• The best way to get the best of an argument is to avoid it.

• It is important not to lose the other person, so always show respect for their opinions.

• Begin in a friendly and amenable way.

• Never say, "You're wrong."

• If you are wrong, admit it quickly and emphatically.

• Let the other person do a great deal of the talking.

• Let them feel that the idea is their own.

• Don't overload others with lots of information. Generally people easily remember a maximum of three things when given information, or given a list or a set of instructions.

• We tend to believe people we like, people who are similar to us, people who are trustworthy and people who have shown expertise. Work on one or all of these points to build your credibility.

• Appeal to the self-interest of the listener. The more personal the benefits, the greater the interest.

• State quantifiable facts rather than opinions. Cite your sources and, when others object, ask specifically for their sources.

• Use anecdotes and stories to make points. These hit both heart and head. Humour acts as a pleasant distracter, making people feel more comfortable. Laughter lowers defences and raises receptivity.

• Objections are standard, so plan your response to the objections you know will probably arise.

• A good tactic is to agree before you disagree. *You're right...* They'll mark you as a reasonable, flexible person.

• When someone pushes, don't push back. As soon as you become aware of this, let up on the pressure. The idea is to neutralise the emotional conflict long enough for logic to take its course. Lower the other's guard with graciousness.

• Repeat, repeat, repeat. If nothing else works, try stating your message in a variety of ways. The listener will eventually get it.

• Empathy is important in communication, and can easily be accessed from a mind that's relaxed.

When I'm in a relaxed state, I am able to put myself in the shoes of another and act from a space of compassion. This doesn't mean that I feel sorry for the other, but that I understand their feelings and can relate to the experience that they are going through.

From this position, I can offer suggestions or give appropriate advice without being drawn into their predicament. This is really the only position from which I can help. Others then, on experiencing this compassionate stance, will be more open and amenable to me and to my position.

The Way of Communication Style

Different people communicate differently. An obvious statement? Yet, it is essential for us to identify the different communication styles used by both ourselves and others, in order for us to develop effective and assertive communication skills. This will help us avoid the perplexity and frustration that can often occur when dealing with the huge variety of individuals who daily cross our path.

There are four behaviour styles that have been identified as ones we are likely to express or experience.

1. Passive communication behaviour is about putting our own personal needs last. It is the doormat syndrome, where we allow ourselves to be trampled on by others. It's not expressing our thoughts or feelings or asking for what we want. Things get bottled up, creating resentment, often resulting in frustrated, angry outbursts.

2. Aggressive communication behaviour style is about trying to dominate, to bully or, even, to humiliate, in order to control and get our own way. It is often characterised by criticising, blaming, attacking or interrupting, often in a forceful, hostile and overbearing manner. It displays low levels of patience and tolerance and is a style that illustrates poor listening skills.

3. Passive-aggressive style is a combination of styles. It avoids direct confrontation (passive), but attempts to get even through various manners of manipulation (aggressive).

This behaviour can be every bit as devastating. The effect of open aggressive behaviour can be likened to being attacked by a bulldozer; while suffering from passive aggression is like being fired at by a sniper: the weapon hits home just as surely.

4. Assertive communication involves clearly expressing what you think, how you feel and what you want, without demanding that you must have things your way. This, then, is clearly a style to be cultivated and worked on in order to succeed in relationships and to create an atmosphere of mutual trust and respect.

The Way of Effective Responses

Challenging, demanding or difficult situations can come leaping out at us like a Jack-in-the-Box, springing up from who-knows-where, with someone saying the most outrageous, angry, thoughtless, stupid, unhelpful, cruel or spiteful things to us.

Yet, if we are aware and prepared, we can turn even these situations into ones with positive outcomes.

Rude, blunt, aggressive or just plain difficult individuals might jump out at us and do a negative Robin Hood, in an attempt to gain the upper ground and control over us.

It is important to train yourself not to respond immediately. Pause for a moment to give yourself time to reflect on what is happening. Work on actually smiling while you ask yourself what the real agenda is of the other and while you choose what stance you are going to take. Keep yourself and your tone calm and controlled. Establish the facts by asking questions and actively listening. Avoid pre-judgements, don't jump to conclusions or reactions too quickly. If things start to become rude and aggressive, here are some possible responses to try:

● **Excuse me, but did you actually say...**

● **Well, I think we've reached the end of this conversation.**

- **Ouch, did you mean to be that rude?**

- **Oh, that's enough about me. What have you been up to?**

- **I'm not sure what your real issue is. What can I do to help?**

Here are some responses we could use in situations where we are confronted with questions that are deliberately positioned to trip us up:

- **If I understand your question correctly, what you're really asking is... then give your own interpretation.**

- **I'm curious why you ask that question.**

- **Your question points to one concern I think...**

It can be very challenging when you are in a meeting, holding the floor and you are confronted by practised interrupters. Here are possible ways to handle this:

Hold your hand up to the interrupter, saying

- **I just have to mention... or Please let me finish or I'll lose my thread (jokey way)**

A conversation with a shy and withdrawn person can also be a demanding and frustrating experience. Having a few questions up your sleeve might just save the day.

- **What would be your perfect day?**

- **How would your best friends describe you?**

- **Have you ever danced in the rain?**

- **If you could live in a book or film, what would it be?**

We have all had to face that dreaded job interview. This can be nerve-racking and stressful at the best of times.

At the end of most interviews, you are generally asked if you have any questions. Well, why not go prepared and put the interviewer under the spotlight?

Asking the right question will tell you a lot about the new situation, whether or not the position is for you, and also show the interviewer that you are discerning and thoughtful.

Here are some suggestions for questions you could ask:

- **What have past employees done to succeed in this position?**

- **What have you enjoyed most about working here?**

- **What are some of the challenges that will face the person filling this position?**

The Way of Subtle Communication

Have you ever been thinking about someone and then, all of a sudden, that person phones you up?

Or, you think of someone you haven't seen for 10 years and suddenly you randomly bump into them in the street?

Is it random, or did you somehow sense it or even create it?

Well, as you are probably aware, we are all connected. It may not seem like that, but on some subtle subconscious level, we are all threaded together. In fact, it is an illusion that we are separate.

On an energetic level, all that we see and touch is just light or energy stored in different forms. When individuals have a strong connection or when the drama in which we are all involved so conspires, seemingly impossible things happen.

It is almost as if we catch a glimpse of the future. But rather than seeing the future, we get a feeling of knowing the future. It may be just a second or two ahead of time, but it is such a strong feeling that we can't deny it. 'Déjà vu' is a good example of this and, if you have ever experienced that, you will know that it is quite spooky.

Thoughts are subtle. What happens to them once they have been thought? As already stated, we live in an energetic universe and a thought travels out into this energy field with a limited form before it is absorbed into the general energy matrix.

From time to time many of us catch such thoughts before their owner has decided to articulate their form. Imagine what a difference we could make with such a subtle ability!

We could naturally feel the pulse of individuals and situations, creating fewer misunderstandings and crossed wires, and with much more empathy and co-operation.

Try this little exercise to help free your mind and allow your own intuitive and subtle subconscious nature to open to the greater energy field of human consciousness.

Let go of stuff that's filling your head at this moment. Step into your inner world. In this inner space, surround yourself with light and silence. Align with that silence.

As thoughts come, do not hold onto them, let them go. Let go of all plans and projections. Allow your mind to be as empty as possible. Stay in the flow, stay with the waves of this vast universal ocean of subtle silent energy.

Experiment with this idea, especially when you are with others, and see what you are observing and feeling. Later, notice if any changes begin to take place within your life or in your awareness.

For our summary affirmation, repeat quietly, slowly, and powerfully to yourself:

When I speak from my heart, I touch the heart and truth of others.

Chapter 7

The Way of Overcoming Stress, Worry and Depression

Stress affects us all in different ways, with different results, and we all have our own ways of responding to it. The accumulated effects of stress, as most of us now realise, are horrendous and life threatening. They range from mental fatigue, anger and depression, to skin problems, the physical effects of cancer, and organ and immune system failures.

It can also lead to emotional, mental and social disabilities that can bring about job loss and relationship breakdown.

One definition of stress is that it is a form of pain that comes bearing the message that something needs to be changed; some lesson needs to be learnt.

The first thing we need to understand is what is creating this stress. We might say it is caused by events or situations or other people. Yet, many people have similar lifestyles and experiences, but not all are adversely affected by them. Why is this?

The main reason for this is that life events themselves don't create stress; it is the mind that creates stress. The issues that we have to contend with are primarily emotional. That means we can choose to create and experience stress, or we can choose not to.

So, it's about taking control and regulating the events and the interactions in which we are involved. Granted, some changes, like the death of a loved one, are out of our control. Yet, the majority of the events we engage in can be selected or not, or they can be spread out and dealt with over time. When an unplanned change occurs, we can choose to over-react, or we can choose to take it in our stride and 'roll with the punches'. If it's impossible to fight or flee from a problem, why not consider flowing with it?

Here are some *Best Ways* to flow with the punches.

The Way of Changing my Response

Stress often originates from the way we think about situations and issues. Things are either *black or white*, with *no shades in between. It's all or nothing. I have to get this 100% perfect.*

We label ourselves*: I'm useless, a failure, unlucky... Or we set unrealistic goals or standards: I must, I should, I have to ...*

Often we blow things up out of all proportion: *This is the end of my career, this is terrible, and it's the end of the world.*

Predicting negative outcomes sabotages us from the start*: I'm going to embarrass myself, everyone's going to laugh at me.* We end up minimising any positive factors in favour of negative aspects.

To equip ourselves to combat stressful situations, we need to challenge these thinking errors. One way of doing this is to examine the evidence for and against these thought statements.

Ask questions like:
What successes have I had?
Is there any other evidence that I am a failure?
When I am thinking sensibly, I can even begin to laugh at my dramatic thought patterns.

Step back and identify the stressor that is creating the stress reaction, and then decide to change the situation.

Reflect on the way you see the situation. Decide to change the *'seeing'* thoughts, so you now *'see'* it differently.

How are you *'feeling'* about the issue? Decide to change the *feelings.*

Reflect on what changes you notice in your body. Decide to release that tension.

What did you do and what was the consequence? OK, now let's decide to use that energy, by taking a different course of action.

The Way of Positive Thought Response

Self-talk can be very helpful and effective in pulling us away from stress precipices, by diffusing and allowing us to take a more resourceful and relaxed approach to life's unfolding dramas. We can use simple self-advice such as:

● **Getting upset won't help.**

● **Easy does it - there's nothing to be gained in getting mad.**

● **I can stay calm and relaxed.**

● **No-one is right, no-one is wrong. We just have different needs.**

● **Stay cool, make no judgements.**

- No matter what is said, I know I'm a good person.

- I can manage this. I'm in control.

- I don't have to take this so seriously.

- I can plan to relax and cope.

- This is funny if I look at it that way.

- Getting stressed, angry and frustrated means it's time to relax and chill.

- I need to take time out, cool off, then come back and deal with it.

- Let me take a deep breath and relax.

- I'll stay calm - and refrain from sarcasm and personal attacks.

- I can't expect people to act the way I want them to.

The Way of Practical Responses

Stress management is about taking responsibility for my own life. It's about stopping the mountain from collapsing, and keeping this avalanche of stuff from overwhelming me. It's carefully assessing and weighing up my priorities and then making a plan to ensure that I achieve them, and to give of my best with the capacities I have at my disposal.

So, why not plan your day, create some order? Be realistic, not superhuman; know your limits of concentration and energy. If possible, take support, learn to delegate and, when necessary, say *"No."* Change your mind-set about your work and work place, find something to enjoy, laugh and have fun at work.

Keep a balance of time between work and play. Keep things in perspective; make time for family and friends as well as work. Manage your health, keep fit and lively. Be a Rolls Royce, not a racing machine. That way you will drive yourself steadily and last longer.

The Way of The Magic Door

If things and issues are getting too much and on top of you, why not try an exercise called
The Magic Door Solution?

Visualise in your mind a doorway. Go through this door and, when you come out the other side, see a beautiful scene... a calm, serene and tranquil lake, bordered by flowers of many colours. It is surrounded by low green hills that softly echo to the sound of flowing streams and singing birds. The sky above is blue and soft and a gentle sun bathes all in its warm embrace. Beside the lake you sit and relax and enjoy this healing, tranquil space. Here you have no worries or concerns, you are at peace. You can stay here as long as you wish. When you feel refreshed, relaxed and peaceful you can return. Now that you have discovered the Magic Door you can return whenever you have a need, whenever you feel worried or stressed. It is available at any time, yet, only you can come through this Magic Door, where worries, concerns and issues are totally forbidden.

The Way of Flowing with Anxiety

Anxiety can be so severe that it becomes completely debilitating.
It's having feelings that something bad or negative is about to happen; feelings of uncertainty and extreme nervousness. It's about being on the edge.

Anything and everything can be a trigger to severe anxiety, creating a state of what is often called living in the *fear of fear*. It brings with it an accompanying adrenaline cascade, which further escalates the feelings of fear, producing intense and seemingly real panic attacks: *I will lose control; I will probably have a heart attack; I might die; I might go mad.*

We can choose several ways to approach anxiety. By using distraction techniques we can sublimate the developing panic. You're in a train or a queue, thoughts begin to flood in, *"I've got to get out of here, I can't stand this."*

At that moment, look at the people around you:

What are they wearing?

Where are they from?
Where are they off to?

Change everything into a fantasy scene.
All are wearing ball gowns, with orange and pink hair. Or even try counting in 5s to 100, sing a nursery rhyme, take out your mobile and play a cartoon that you've already primed for this occasion.

Try postponing your anxiety or worry as opposed to suppressing it. Instead of reacting and responding to these thoughts as they emerge, note the concern, and create a specific time and location when you will return to deal with them.

Gradually, over time, this method becomes easier and you'll be able to manage your anxieties and worries in a more relaxed frame of mind. Away from trigger situations, they will seem less intense and problematic. Deep breathing is always extremely helpful. Taking deep slow breaths from the lower abdomen, holding for 3 or 4 seconds and allowing a slow release, can considerably reduce anxiety symptoms.

The Way of the Balloon Ride

Visualisations connected to an affirmed intention can also be a very effective support. Try this **balloon exercise**:

You're walking along a country lane and you turn into a field. It is wide and spacious with one or two small trees. It is a pleasant and relaxing scene. In the middle of the field is a large and colourful balloon tethered to its basket by several ropes. You walk over. A sign on the basket says, "Welcome," and so you climb into the balloon. You untie the ropes and allow the balloon to lift from the ground. Slowly, gently your balloon gains height. You look below and see the fields and houses becoming smaller and smaller. As you gain further height, everything becomes quiet and very peaceful. Feel this quiet and enjoy this space. The higher you go the more there is a feeling of great tranquillity. You have left below your old worries and concerns. Here there are no other thoughts, just feelings of lightness and peaceful serenity. Whenever you wish, you can return, but right now, you are filled with an experience of peaceful well-being.

The balloon exercise can be used in many situations: at work, out walking, or even in company. A switch of focus and you're in your balloon. Others may see you and your smiling face, but your thoughts are with you in your balloon.

A major cause of worries, anxiety and heaviness is that we think too much. We worry about the future, about what we did in the past, am I doing the right thing now?

Our inner world of silence can help us get out of these cul-de-sacs. Just stand back, let go of and look at the problem. Is it really there or have I created it?

Look deeply into it and you'll suddenly see it is not increasing.

In fact it is decreasing.

It is becoming smaller and smaller. The more you put your energy into observation, the smaller it becomes. And the moment comes when suddenly it is not there.

The Way of Flowing with Depression

Depression is a serious mood disorder that certainly makes it tough to function and to enjoy life. It brings states and feelings of hopelessness, apathy, emptiness and despair, and can cause insomnia, extreme fatigue, and a loss of energy and concentration. Different factors may be their cause, yet, what keeps all of them going can often be how we deal with these effects.

Let's look at different ways we can change our life set-up. Let's try and change tack and create a different energy input and mental outlook.

Increasing our exercise levels and becoming more active will certainly have a big impact on our moods. Go for regular walks, go to the gym, cycle and swim. Engage in a hobby. Why not find an old interest, revive it and rediscover it's fun element. What have you thought about but not got round to doing?

Pamper yourself, do something you really enjoy doing or do something relaxing and calming.

When you notice that a wave of depression is starting to come, a useful strategy that you can use to help counter it is to focus your attention elsewhere; that is, become aware of other things, being mindful of their presence.

Depression and the Way of Mindful-Awareness

Try the following as an example of mindful-awareness.

Become aware of the room and its contents. Notice, without judgement or association, the shapes and colours and the light. Become aware of the sounds and the silence beneath these sounds. Be aware of your breathing, the slow intake and the slow release of this life-giving energy. Notice your body, how it sits, how your legs and arms are positioned. Feel the chair you are sitting on, its texture and form. Focus on one thing in the room. Just rest your gaze without comparing, judging or associating for a minute or so. Now observe your thoughts as they come and as they go. What emotions do you notice are coming to you?

Mindful awareness brings us into the present, where there are no ghosts from the past or projections into the future. From this place of observation, we can make adjustments, gain perspective and control by choosing a different emotional path.

Depression creates a down-in-the-dumps attitude, making us feel miserable and producing a self-image and self-esteem that's rock bottom. So let's challenge and change the way we think about ourselves and others and the world.

Learn to notice your strengths and qualities, and the things you do well. Make a list of what you have achieved, what you know about, what you are good at. List evidence that people like you, the compliments you have received, the times you helped others. Write down your three main qualities and how they help you.

Recall your abilities:

I can stay calm in a crisis.
I'm normally well organized.
I always have time for friends.

They say I'm humorous and funny, I'm a very good listener.

Struggling with problems can often bring us down. Try stepping back, letting go for a moment, then clearly asking: Is it such a big issue? Is there another way of looking at this problem? OK, what steps do I need to take? Maybe write down some solutions, then choose the most suitable for you to use. It is helpful to remember that not all problems are solvable by us! Consider who else could help in this instance.

The Way of Affirmations

Affirmations of positive well-being are very powerful in helping to restore and strengthen our self-esteem. Try using and applying some of the following and go on to create your own:

● **I am beautiful just the way I am.**

● **I love and respect myself unconditionally.**

● **I love the world and the world loves me.**

- **I do not have to prove myself worthy of anything, to anyone.**

- **I am able, capable and intelligent; I can resolve the problems that come my way.**

- **I remind myself that no-one can affect me unless I let them.**

- **I am constantly growing, evolving and creating a wonderful version of myself.**

- **Every day, in every way, I'm getting better and better.**

- **All is well, everything is working out for my highest good and I am safe.**

You'll be surprised how effective these powerful self-teaching tools are; this is inner guidance for the mind, enabling us to over-ride our old negative programming, taking us confidently and positively forward.

The Way of Nature

Another helpful and uplifting exercise that will give us a bigger picture, a new and wider perspective, is to see the beauty and wonder of nature. See the flowers, their colours and beauty, the trees, full of majesty and strength. See nature's naturalness, benevolence and ordered calm, and relate it to yourself. We can use such thoughts as these affirmations:

● **I am like a cloud, often full of negative thoughts, denying myself the clear and open sky. Yet, in letting them go, I discover a new and positive landscape.**

● **I am like the Sun, whose light is often shielded by cloud and dark, yet, all things pass and I will still remain a shining light.**

● **I am like a field. The thoughts I sow yield either flowers of subtle fragrance or weeds of thorny bramble.**

● **I am like a feather, weightless and light and soft, separated and free. I am able to hold, to ride the wind of changing circumstance.**

Let these and similar thoughts work on your mood and mindset. Observe, appreciate and notice nature's harmony, its unity, its collective acceptance of its many parts.

Experiment being in the midst of this natural world, try to be still, have no thoughts, harmonise with its vibration, be one with this feeling.

For our concluding affirmation, remember again to use the three step approach:

Accept. Experience. Become.

Affirmation:

**I am peaceful,
Centred in peace,
Surrounded by peace.**

Chapter 8

The Way of Happiness

Happiness is quite difficult to define, yet, most people are aware of whether they are happy or not. Certainly happiness is not pleasure, which is fleeting: parties, receiving a gift, a day on the beach, or, as bidden by myths of the consumerist world, the accumulation of things that we run after to recreate imagined states of bliss. Chasing pleasure is not happiness.

Happiness is a feeling of contentment, when your life is just as it should be, when your life fulfils all its needs. So what are our needs? What does it take to achieve happiness?

You can be happy, you should be happy and you can choose to be happy.

Here are some *Best Ways* to bring you into the sunlight of real inner happiness.

The Way of Being Your Self

There's nothing more uncomfortable than wearing shoes that don't fit. The same goes for identity.

Copying behaviours or cloning what others are like just doesn't work. Influenced by the culture of labels and personality, we try to make a composite personality, pieced together from those we admire, hoping it will open the doors to success and happiness. Unfortunately, when I'm not being myself, it soon becomes evident to all and sundry, and eventually to me also, that I'm a fake.

I have to tell myself;

**I am unique,
I have ability, capability and talent.**

Those who have achieved happiness and success first believed in themselves.

I can only be who I am.

I can only play the cards that I am dealt.

Happiness and contentment is based on this self-acceptance, being who I am, being real and authentic.

Life becomes immensely more comfortable and enjoyable when we are able to live with ourselves, sharing and speaking from our hearts about what we think and what we believe. By being who you are, your real and authentic self begins to formulate, and soon you and the world discover that you are very special indeed!

The Way of Giving

On recalling times when we gave gifts, didn't we feel good? Wasn't there something magical as we watched the faces of those who received them? Giving makes us happier and healthier.

Giving is the real receiving. We enjoy it, it activates all our body's feel-good chemicals and emotions.

Increase your acts of kindness whenever you can. Do things for others, offer support or advice, make someone smile, pay a compliment, help someone who is struggling, let others know you care.

Giving can also include listening. Listening gives others space and time to share. It is co-operating with another's idea while putting yours on the back burner for the time being.

Experiment in giving in all areas of your life and watch the barometer of your happiness rise rapidly.

The Way of Appreciating

We live in a wonderful and beautiful world, yet, we spend most of our time unaware, nose down, like grazing sheep.

Take time out, look around, notice and appreciate the wonder of the world around us.

Breathe, take in the incredible multiplicity of life forms, the colours, the fragrances. Look at the majestic trees, enjoy the smell of things like grass and coffee.

What happens then is that we move our focus away from concerns about the future, we stop dwelling on the past, we stop thinking and worrying about the non-essentials, our spirits become lifted and we are able to get more out of our day-to-day living. The world changes because we see it as a different place and we begin to participate in life's great joys.

The Way of Developing Positive Emotions

Over time our innate and positive natural responses have been overlaid and subverted by the manifold influences that constantly assail us from all sides. From family, friends and teachers, to the ever-present voice of the media and the consumerist world, we are presented with doom-and-gloom scenarios;

If we fail, don't achieve, don't become, don't match up, don't purchase...

And, of course, it's inevitable that we will fail or not achieve. We then hold onto these fears and failures, these lacks and losses.
Our bright and happy little sun that shone so gaily becomes shrouded by the dark and heavy clouds of fear and negative feelings and emotions.

To help and heal our hurting inner child, we must learn to create positive emotions of joy, gratitude, contentment, inspiration and pride. We need to do things that make us feel good, things that we want to do, not things that were part of our earlier programmed success package.

Things like listening to music or watching funny films. Try smiling in a serious place, saying something funny or having a good laugh, then watch the reaction you get.

Don't look back as you continue on this upward spiral of positive energy.

Be realistic. Yes, there will be ups and downs, but just keep focusing on the good and positive aspects.

The Way of Creating New Experiences

Life can often seem flat, with little bubble or fizz. Maybe you're bored or feel stuck. To bring back that enthusiasm, exuberance and satisfaction you may need to change things around or do something different, something new and interesting.

You might need to remove something from your life that doesn't really work for you, to make room for something better and more rewarding.

Focus, not on something you don't want to do, but on things that you do want to do, on things you love.

Go for that thing that you said you always wanted to do. Learn that language that you keep talking about. Develop new skills. Learn to cook in a new way.

Change your route to work, your style of clothing. Visit a place you've never visited before.

Say yes to something you've always said no to. Take ballet lessons, give blood, learn tai chi. Volunteer at your local hospital or hospice. Hang out with people who are compatible with you, who are positive and like-minded.

By keeping yourself engaged, constantly curious and becoming a committed lifelong learner, you'll feel a great sense of accomplishment, self-confidence and resilience, making yourself happier and more satisfied.

The Way of Finding Meaning and Purpose

Apathy, boredom or being unaware can sink your boat, even before you leave the harbour of your life's journey. As with any journey, there has to be a purpose and a direction. We need to know where we are going. A life with purpose fills you with energy and drive.

Nothing can be a drag; you're doing things that are worthwhile.

When you have a purpose, you create a more meaningful life. Purpose helps you decide what you stand for and enables you to see your place in the world. Purpose helps you focus and move forward. You feel you have value and significance, which bring well-being, satisfaction and happiness.

The question is, how can we discover our purpose, especially when we have so many disparate voices bidding us to do this and that?

It's easy to follow what others are doing, but, of course, what is necessarily appropriate for one person may well be totally inappropriate for another. We have to find our own path.

To get a clear picture, you need to disengage from surrounding influences and pressures. Use the clarity of silence, by first stepping back and reflecting on what it is that you value.

What qualities for you are important in others, in relationships? What type of a life do you wish for? What type of life do you value?

Then ask yourself what it is that you want to go for, what it is that you want to achieve. Make a decision and go for it.

Create some goals, some stepping stones – and you're on your way. You have aligned with what you believe in, what you value.

Your journey is now one of integrity and truth. With your purpose set, your life is happier, you feel more in control, there is less stress and anxiety, and you and others and life in general don't seem that bad at all.

The Way of Empowering Your Day

Getting through the day can be exhausting and stressful and, just as it finishes and we're seeing some light at the end of the tunnel, the spectre of the following day looms and all again is darkness.

However, we can overcome this treadmill state by changing our attitude and mindset, whereby our day can become one of value, learning and satisfaction.

Why not start the day by refreshing your mind, having some silence, filling yourself with light and energy, and with the positive intention that on this day you will learn and experience new and wonderful things, that you will meet and connect with amazing and incredible people.

We will certainly need a strategy to deal with the variety of responses that will come our way. Let's accept that each one of us is interpreting the world according to our own present state of consciousness and in the best ways we are able. So why not accept and appreciate with good wishes and best feelings each one's input, each one's part. Our day will then flow in harmony with greater well-being.

Yet, dealing with difficult people is always challenging, so sometimes it's necessary to have a more focused and strategic approach.

Being proactive with such individuals will always be more successful. List their qualities. Ask what you can learn from them, what they are teaching you and what you need to give to this person? You can then turn things around.

Empowering your day is also about recharging and renewing your depleted energies. Don't wait until you're running on near empty.

Every hour take time out to stop, to go into silence for a few moments and to let go of everything and to experience yourself as a being of light and peace and love.

Affirm to yourself:

**I am free, serene and calm.
I drift on a sea of wonderful tranquillity.
I refresh my mind and total being with these energies.**

How we are in the morning has a lot to do with the night before. We often wake up in the morning just as exhausted as we were when we went to sleep.

The thoughts, emotions and feelings of the interactions of the day are often still active in our subconscious as we sleep, continuing to drain us. We need to put them to sleep, to close them down. A few selected thoughts will do this just before sleep.

I separate myself from the thoughts and activities of the day.
I let them all drift away in the soft stream of silence.
There is now just a state of rest.
I return to the world of peace and light.
In a state of freedom and release.

Let us affirm and experience:

Affirmation:

I smile, feeling content and satisfied, as I make myself full. I am then able to put the needs of others before my own.

Chapter 9

The Way of Overcoming Anger

Anger is omnipresent in our society, from road rage to the soaring incidence of child physical abuse. Everyone is touched by it. In recent times, tens of thousands have had and are having therapy, as they struggle with their overwhelming bouts of anger that are destroying their lives and badly affecting others, and leaving them with the deep scar residues of regret, loss, hurt and fear.

Anger emerges from many sources, not only from the here and now, like when somebody steps on your toes or wrongs and criticises you. Its roots can be traced back to earlier times when you were hurt, abused or neglected. The pain was something you carried year after year. It may have left deep wounds inside you – so now it's hard to feel safe or loved or worthy.

Sometimes it doesn't take much provocation to trigger those feelings of being unloved, unworthy or unsafe, and the anger rises up right alongside that old pain

I think it is important to get one thing straight: You aren't to blame because you struggle with anger. You aren't a bad person because you forget to be cool and calm. Rather, you are a person in pain – whether chronic or occasional – when it hits like a wave which totally overwhelms you and drives you into a state of mind in which nothing else matters but expressing what you feel. Anger is a way of coping, helping temporarily to overcome the hurt and helplessness, giving the illusion that you're in control. That's why it is hard to manage.

When we try to cork it, we can often feel more acute pain. So it's time for us to stop blaming and kicking ourselves; it really doesn't help, it just creates more pain.

Here are important truths about anger and *Best Steps* of overcoming anger.

Understanding the Effects of Anger

The payback of anger can be huge. Anger absorbs a great deal of mental energy. It creates a kind of heavy cloak of turbulent cloud that seems to hang constantly around the mind, clouding our thinking, making it hard to concentrate, to see the bigger picture or to generally enjoy life. All that seems to be with us is the peace-less-ness of worry and agitation. It can also lead to stress, depression and other mental health problems.

Anger also has a very damaging effect on our health. It creates high levels of stress and hypertension, making us susceptible to heart disease, diabetes, high cholesterol, a weakened immune system, insomnia and high blood pressure

Another major consequence can be the damage it does to relationships, family and friends, causing lasting scars in the people we love most. When chronic intense anger is expressed, it makes it hard for people to trust us, speak honestly or feel comfortable – they never know what is going to set us off or what we might do.

Angry people often end up feeling painfully disconnected from others. It can cut them off from social support, often creating in them a cynical attitude towards others so they are unable to recognise support even when it is available.

Angry people are often unable to appreciate help and support when it is offered, no matter how sincere others may be.

They often become unrealistic and demanding in their expectations, making all available support seem not good enough. So they keep others at arm's length, thus receiving less support and increasing the deep-down feeling of isolation and loneliness.

Career-wise, outbursts of anger and lashing out not only alienate colleagues, supervisors or clients, eroding respect and trust, but they also create a negative reputation which can follow you wherever you go, making it very difficult to get ahead.

Untangling the Myths about Anger

Often anger can be extolled as healthy... *It's good to let it all out! Shows you care, you're inspirational, passionate, a good motivator.* It can seem an attractive or sensible choice. So let's examine some of these illusions of anger.

Anger reduces stress

After an outburst, you're more relaxed, a weight has been lifted from your shoulders and you can breathe again. The downside of this approach is that the stress will come back with a vengeance. Using anger will create more anger and each time it will become harder to control. Your anger becomes worse and so does the anger of others towards you.

Anger blocks and hides our emotional pain

Anger can put a tight lid on painful emotions. If you get mad enough you can block out fears, loss, guilt, shame and feelings of rejection or failure. This is a short term pay-off with long-term consequences.

By not letting yourself experience these feelings, you ignore important signals offering guidance for something that you may need to do or stop doing. Maybe a good reason to allow yourself to feel guilt is because you need to face up to or to do something about the issue.

These guilty feelings will only get increasingly worse over time. To alleviate the damage, you have to address the issue now.

Anger gets people's attention

Through shouting and yelling, people will listen and pay attention. This can only be a very short-term strategy. Some may listen, some may run, most will eventually tune out and not respond.

They will try to avoid you and, worse still, hold it against you.
With the constant use of theatrical anger, people become inured and hardened to it, resenting you and, in the end, they shut down.

Anger as a tool to teach

When others fail to produce, let you down or just screw up, an inner rage wants to punish them, to teach them a lesson.

All that matters is that they feel the pain you are feeling, that they feel your disappointment. Yet, each time you act out these impulses, you make enemies and often they are the people you love and need most. Naturally then your enemies will want to punish you! We see how we can push each other into new excesses of rage and aggression.

Anger can help you change others

In dysfunctional relationships, we learn to use anger to extort things from each other, we coerce with blow-ups – or the fear of blow-ups – into compliance.

Anger is used as a controlling club. In the short term, it can often give you what you want. In the long term, people turn off and turn away from you.

People resent being controlled, as do you. You will be left alone and helpless

10 Best Steps on Overcoming Anger

1. Recognising First Signs
Don't do anything. Don't act on the angry feeling. This is just an emotion. You can feel it without turning it into a behaviour.

2. Response
Try to step back from this feeling and label it, seeing that it is, in fact, separate from you. Notice its strength and how it pushes you into action. Accept that it's there. There's nothing wrong with anger, it's only a signal that you're in pain. It's only a problem when you act on it and you then hurt yourself or others.

3. Become an Observer
Don't push the angry feeling away, but at the same time, don't hold onto it.
It comes like a wave, building, cresting and then slowly receding. Let it come and then let it go. Watch as it grows and diminishes as if you're a scientist observing a phenomenon.

4. Keeping Things Small

Try not to amplify your anger; don't dwell on the unfairness of the situation. Don't review past failings of the individual and rehearse in your mind events leading up to your anger. Just notice and accept the feelings, watching as it gradually diminishes.

5. Managing your Body Language

Breathe out for longer than you breathe in and relax as you breathe out. This will calm you down effectively and help you think more clearly. Smile instead of frowning, this releases endorphins. Speak slowly rather than loudly, even go overboard on this, make your voice almost soothing. Relax your body as opposed to tightening up.

6. Controlled Expression

As soon as you're thinking clearly, express your frustration in an assertive but non-confrontational way. State your concerns and needs clearly and directly, without hurting others or trying to control them.

7. Language of Control

To avoid criticising or placing blame, which will only increase tension, use 'I' statements to describe the problem. Be respectful and specific. For example, say, *"I'm upset that you discussed the issue with Tom before consulting with me."* Try to avoid phrases that include: *always, never, should or shouldn't, must or mustn't, ought or oughtn't.*

8. Approaches to the Circumstances

Rather than go in for the attack, why not try disengaging; look away, walk away. Make no comment about the provoking situation. Save it for another time maybe, now will only blow the issue up further. Or, try empathising rather than judging; be mildly supportive, "I can see you're concerned and upset..."
It may sound a little phoney, but better than alternatively wanting to hit them over the head with a plank.

9. Use of Humour

Lightening up can help diffuse tension.

Use humour to help you face what's making you angry and to let go of any unrealistic expectations you have for how things should go. Avoid sarcasm though, it can hurt feelings and make things worse.

10. Practise Relaxation Skills
When your anger flares, you can put your relaxation skills to work. This is the time to practise deep breathing exercises or to turn on a pre-prepared imaginary relaxing scene in the mind... An example of such a scene could sound like the following:

I see myself peacefully walking along the seashore. Above there is a soft, hazy orange sun, set high in a clear blue sky. I stroll on the soft, yellow sands by the lapping water's edge. Looking out to the calm, still ocean, mirrored still and clear, my thoughts are drawn into the unlimited vastness of that serene tranquillity and I feel at peace, in harmony, at one with all.

You might also repeat a calming word or phrase such as:

I am peaceful, calm and light
Stay calm
Relax
Take it easy
I can handle it
I can't change this person
7654321...I'm now stopped, still and calm

You might also listen to music, write in a journal, do some exercises, or go for a walk... Whatever it takes to encourage relaxation.

Affirmation; stepping back, I slowly repeat to yourself, and bring into your awareness:

I understand that the anger that comes is a signal, a sign of my inner pain. I stand back, observing it like a wave rising, cresting and slowly diminishing. I let it go.

Chapter 10

The Way of Meditation

Meditation is the experience of empowerment. It's about stepping into our inner world and connecting with our subtle energies, qualities and powers. This empowerment changes our nature, attitude and consciousness.

It promotes physical and mental calm, relaxation and peacefulness, together with clarity and awareness, enabling the mind to think clearly and freely. It's the strength that gets things done.

Meditation works with the energy field of spiritual light. Let us now explore and experience the three main stages and *Best Ways* of meditation.

1
First Stage:
Spiritual Self Awareness:

Spiritual self-awareness is about the acceptance and experience of ourselves as spiritual light energy. We need to hold this awareness with either our thoughts or feelings, or to visualise ourselves as this subtle light and then to affirm this understanding to ourselves. Let us practise this:

I am light,

I am spiritual and eternal,

I am a being of subtle energy.

Repeat this affirmation three times.

As we say it the first time, we simply accept it.

When we say it the second time, we integrate it, by saying it slowly, with feeling, experiencing each word.

In the third time of saying it, we hold the experience, the feelings. We don't think, connect or associate. We just be with that state.

Practise with patience and gradually the meditation will hold.

2
Second Stage:
Emerging Your Power:

Now that we have re-connected with our original spiritual self, we can emerge and experience our natural, spiritual nature, which is like a reservoir, a core centre of spiritual energy. Once linked, we release its energy like a beautiful inner fountain of qualities and powers into our experiential life.

Let's experience this 2nd Stage

Using the vehicle of thought, we will emerge and experience our original, primal nature:

Let us slowly affirm to ourselves:

My nature is of love,

I am that love.

My nature is of peace,

I am that peace.

My nature is of light,

I am that light.

Again, as we did for the first affirmation, repeat the meditations slowly, feeling and experiencing each of the qualities.

And thirdly, repeat again, but holding and being that feeling, allowing yourself to be that love, to be that peace, to be that light.

3
Third Stage:
Transformation:

Now the mind has become subtle and stabilised through the first two stages, we are able to centre our thoughts on the unlimited light of the Supreme. Focused and connected to this immense body of spiritual light, our newly emergent energies are held, recharged and regenerated. We become transformed.

Let us experience this change.

Let us affirm:

Centred In the light of the Supreme, I rest my mind.

Centred In the light of the Supreme, I am recharged.

Centred In the light of the Supreme, I am empowered.

After first affirming, we again slowly experience this power and then we stay stabilised, centred within this great and powerful energy.

In meditation, we are reframing our awareness; we are re-sourcing our power; our energies and our qualities become activated, purified and empowered.

The Way of Meditation on the Move

One of the specialities of meditation is that it can be experienced in any situation or place in which you find yourself. Be it for a need to remain calm, to cope with a testing situation or to tap into some clarity, all it requires is a few seconds, a switch of consciousness, a mental step back from the issue and then a click into your meditation energy field.

Most of our day-to-day activities and interactions drain and sap our strength and energy reserves.
Yet, we can always find free moments, spaces where we can use the meditation experience to refresh and empower ourselves, and replace and regenerate our lost energies.

Sitting at our desk, travelling by bus, train or plane, even whilst driving, the mind can become relaxed, focused and so more tuned to the task or journey ahead.

Let's experiment with the types of possible thoughts we can bring into our active, moving meditations.

I would suggest that we keep our affirmations simple. Use just what is needed at the time. Also you may, or may not, like to use a visual symbol to help hold the experience, such as seeing yourself surrounded by the light energy of the quality you are experiencing:

I am light...

I am peace...

I am calm...

I am love...

I am the observer...

(seeing what's needed for the steps ahead)

The Way of Meditation as a Support

Meditation is a very effective and powerful tool to help and support us in our day-to-day interactions and connections with others.

We have seen how meditation relaxes and focuses our thinking, sharpens our awareness and insight, and empowers us with spiritual inner qualities which are necessary in all relationships and dealings with others.

Regular practise of meditation changes our old negative and reactive nature, replacing it with new positive qualities and subtle powers. Each practice becomes more and more manifest and evident in our personality.

It integrates, becomes part of us.
These subtle energies then start to work for us automatically.

Our personality becomes amenable, easy, light and co-operative. Others find us easy to work with and enjoy our company. We become nicer people.

Such change soon becomes evident to everyone, as they experience our openness, our enthusiasm and smiling face. A more subtle change happens with our vibrational energy. This is what people meet before they actually physically engage with us.

Our vibrational energy field is what first connects with people and intuitively tells them what type of person we are. This can't be faked.

The meditation experience repairs and reinforces our subtle energy body.
Each meditation fills this energy body with light, healing and new power which surrounds us, protecting and communicating. In connection, it reaches out, disarming fears, worries and any anxieties that others may have about us. It is subtly telling others we're OK, we're to be trusted.

The Way of Creating Atmosphere and Influencing

In meditation, we create our own personal atmosphere, which, as we have seen, surrounds and protects us. Yet, the influence doesn't just stop with ourselves. When opening up our awareness, we can easily affect the surrounding atmosphere. When we have thoughts of peace and are centred in peace, these thought vibrations can rapidly change the atmosphere of the room, the workplace or where we live.

Meditation can not only change the atmosphere of a location, but will also most certainly influence those who come into contact with that vibration.
Creating the atmosphere directly through meditation or projecting it to a focused location will greatly help and uplift others who might be struggling with worries and negativity.

The Way of Centring in a Globe of Light

Here are a few thoughts that you could use:

I centre myself in a globe of purest light. It is the light of peace, it is the light of love. From here I send pure thoughts of pure vibration, of purest love to touch all hearts, all minds, for this is the energy, the power of true feelings, changing the atmosphere. It is the vibration, helping to give support, helping others to forget and forgive and move into well-being and into harmony.

The Way of Meditating to Empower

Throughout the day, we have to make numerous decisions, satisfy many different demands and occasionally deal with upsets and disappointments.

Here are some ideas and suggestions that you might like to use in your meditations:

Once again, I use the process of visualisation and affirmation when I need some determination, and strong resolve to face an issue or difficulty. Visualise a tall mighty mountain and affirm to yourself:

I am like a mountain,
Strong, powerful and stable.
Nothing can shake or disturb me.

Hold and experience this for as long as you can manage.

The Way of Meditating to Relax and Uplift Myself

When I need some peace and calm or when coping with an upset, I visualise a beautiful, tranquil lake and affirm:

I am like a lake,
Still and peaceful and calm.

Hold this experience and allow yourself to be integrated into its energy.

When I feel a little low and despondent, I can boost my confidence and self-esteem by visualising a house, all closed and shuttered. Now I open the shutters and switch on the lights. Everywhere is filled with light and freshness and I affirm:

I am like the house. I open all the windows and doors of my life that have been formerly closed.
I switch on the light of inner awareness. I see my uniqueness, my qualities and special role.
I now open and engage with the beauty of life. I see and accept all things for what they are. I now experience the beautiful energy of natural harmony and spiritual well-being.

To enhance or change my attitude;

I visualise a majestic, flowering and abundant tree.

I am like a tree,
Open, unselfish, always giving,
Always sharing.

The Way of Meditating to Clarify

When things are getting on top of me and I need some space, some clarity, I visualise an image of a bird gliding gracefully through the air and affirm to myself:

I am like a bird, free ,light and detached, sailing high above the things below.

Experience it, hold it, be it.
Using these affirmations, and creating your own, will give you much needed respite and relaxation.

They'll energise, change and free your thinking, and refresh your attitude. Exploding this positivity bomb immediately affects and uplifts the atmosphere, influencing all those whom you meet.

Affirmation of spiritual power:

**I am light. all are light,
God is light, there is nothing but light.**

Chapter 11

The Best 3 Questions

At this point, we would like to ask *you 3 Best* questions.

Q: How much do you value your happiness? Are you prepared to have it taken away from you by your own mind?

Q: Have you begun to accept that you are not actually your mind? Do you see that it is your mind that has been giving you the run-around, playing pranks on you, and generally getting up to mischief for quite some time now?

Q: Are you ready to take back your power and no longer be sub-servient to the deception of your thinking? Are you ready to relax your mind?

It's worth spending some quiet time with yourself really looking at these three questions.

After all, who's in charge here? Is it you who is in charge? Is it you, the conscious living being, the creator of your own destiny, the master of your future and the designer of your journey, who is in charge? Or, is it the part of you that is chattering in the background of your mind?

The mind, as previously mentioned, is our most powerful tool. It can be our greatest ally and, yet, it is often our greatest foe.

The mind can generate materials of beauty and structures of incredible complexity, or it can become a weapon of self-destruction and self-betrayal. When we hurt ourselves, we also hurt the ones we love, the ones who are closest to us, the ones we should be encouraging and supporting.

Once we choose to relax our minds, there is a doorway that opens up, like a portal into unlimited possibilities, creating a chance to make a difference.

This pathway of opportunity can influence our ongoing journey and redesign the landscape of our perception. Seize the moment.

If not now, then never.

When we are able to relax our minds, we become free. Free to love, free to express and free to be. Free to be who we truly are and to allow others to be who they are.

Conclusion

In every situation, in every part of our waking day, we need to be in a state of calm, relaxed alertness.

Such is the frantic and frenetic state of life these days that it seems we are constantly and always in the middle of some maelstrom of colliding events and issues; pressures, decisions and choices are always knocking on our door.

There never seems a moment when we are not facing something or another. Invariably it becomes all too wearing and exhausting. We either run for the hills, tune out and hope it all goes away, or we resolutely face the onslaught.

Sometimes we successfully cope or deal with the issue, or we are overrun by the runaway train of these ever-present matters. And yet, in the next blink of an eyelid and barely recovered, we are again facing a new bombardment of concerns and problems. It starts to become all too much.

Yet, we have a solution, a way to win against, what seem at times, unfair odds.

Due to all the stuff going on around us, most of us have been distracted and have forgotten our own unique and powerful inner qualities and abilities.

So rather than just letting circumstances hit us full on, and then trying to understand, resolve and get some clear water, we can deal with things in a very different way.

Through silence, we can find ways to resolve these often very difficult situations that life keeps throwing up at us at an alarmingly frequent rate.

Silence enables us to step back, slow down and think clearly. A clear mind then can assimilate the factors of the situation, process it and help us make an effective decision on ways forward.

Silence gives us space to avoid reactional behaviour and rash decisions. It enables us to connect with our inner resources of virtues and spiritual energy, so linking us with intuitive and more subtle perceptive thinking.

Our life, our relationships, our work and our world, then become easier and more peaceful. Co-operation, harmony and acceptance become a more natural part of our everyday living.

In these difficult and changing times, if you want to truly thrive and survive, you will need to understand, *How to Relax Your Mind*, and we sincerely hope that, *The 10 Best Ways*, can help you to achieve this.

If you like the thoughts and ideas in this little book, then tell a friend, and pass it on...

Collectively, we will change the world, by changing ourselves...

ACKNOWLEDGMENTS

Special thanks to Leza,
who has helped to
shape the spirit
of the words within
this book, and make
it beautiful.

Thanks also to Lynn
and Davina for
their attentive eyes.

Finally,
eternal thanks
to all those guides
and teachers that
helped us on our
Way.

http://www.eternalpointoflight.com

Made in the USA
Charleston, SC
19 July 2016